Elephant

America's #1 Business Coach
Provides the Proven Playbook On

HOW TO BUILD A SUCCESSFUL BUSINESS

Featuring 50+ Claymations, Words of Wisdom & Super
Moves You Can Use Special Edition

It's not about where you came from or what kind
of car you are driving today. It's about where you
are going. I started my entrepreneurial journey
inside a 1998 Ford Escort.

"Don't read this book unless you are passionate about becoming financially
successful while simultaneously creating both time and financial freedom.
I'll teach you the systems but you must supply the B.O.O.M.! (the BIG,
OVERWHELMING, OPTIMISTIC, MOMENTUM)."

~ Clay Clark

How to Build a Successful Business:
Elephant in the Room Special Edition

ISBN: 979-8-9925935-1-8
Copyright © by Clay Clark

Clay Clark Publishing
3920 West 91st Street South
Tulsa, OK 74132

CONTENTS

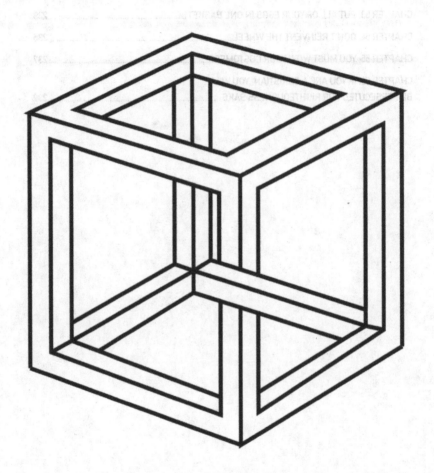

"This picture is complicated. Your path
to success does not need to be."

- Clay Clark

WELCOME TO ELEPHANT IN THE ROOM

"When providing value to a customer. You want your offer to be so good and so irresistible that people simply cannot say no to it. Your goal must be to WOW your customers!"

-DOCTOR ROBERT ZOELLNER

(Long-time Clay Clark friend, mentor, the former employer of Clay Clark's wife Vanessa Clark and the self-made entrepreneur and Tulsa-based success story that built the www.DrZoellner.com optometry clinics, the www.Z66AA.com auto auction, and the man who teamed up with Sean Kouplen to save and turn-around The Bank of Nowata while transforming it into the thriving www.RegentBank.com.)

Welcome to Elephant In The Room, I'm beyond glad that you found us or that we found you. I hope that this book and your experience at Elephant In The Room Men's Grooming Lounge will provide you with a positive and uplifting escape from the daily jackassary that we all experience around us. I created Elephant In The Room to provide you with the very best men's grooming experience Oklahoma has to offer while providing you with a relaxing environment where great guys like you can enjoy uplifting conversations while being surrounded in an atmosphere and decor that is rustic, man-focused, and positive. I have obsessively designed each store with a focus on WOWing you and to create the "man cave" we all want to have. I am writing this book for you because I sincerely desire to improve your life (if only by 1%).

"Clay Clark is my second favorite son."

MARY CLARK

(Clay Clark's mom.)

"We've met some of the biggest CEOs in the world, guys that run the biggest Fortune 500 companies and Clay Clark has 100 times the backbone of the toughest person that you will see."

ERIC TRUMP

(The Executive Vice President of The Trump Organization who is responsible for managing the $8 billion business, thousands of employees, the Trump Organization's real estate and the Trump brands.)

"Five years ago, I just felt like we were stuck, so I reached out to Clay Clark. Clay Clark helped me to build the systems we have now!"

GABE SALINAS

(Founder of the WindowNinjas.com franchise)

"Clay, you've become an influencer. More than anything else, you have evolved into an influencer where your word has more and more power. As you know, there are a lot of fake influencers out there. I'm glad that you and I agree so much. You are on it, man! Everybody listen to this guy. He knows what he's talking about."

ROBERT KIYOSAKI

(The best-selling author of The Rich Dad Poor Dad book series and a man who has sold over 40 million copies of his entrepreneur books)

"We have grown 5X! We have grown from 60 to 300 employees. Before we teamed up with Clay Clark, we didn't have any systems or processes!"

KEVIN THOMAS

(Founder of MultiClean.com)

"Clay Clark is an entrepreneur extraordinaire."

DAVID ROBINSON

(NBA Hall of Basketball Player, former NBA MVP, NBA Championship Winner & Investor)

"Clay Clark has helped us grow from 2 locations to now 6 locations. Clay has done a great job of navigating anything that has to do with running the business, building the systems, the checklists, the workflows, the audits, how to navigate lease agreements, how to buy property, how to work with brokers and builders. This guy is just amazing."

CHARLES COLAW

(Founder of ColawFitness.com)

"He's like Steve Martin meets Steve Forbes."

JIM STOVALL

(New York Times best-selling self-help writer best known for his bestselling novel The Ultimate Gift. The book was made into the movie The Ultimate Gift, distributed by 20th Century Fox. The Ultimate Gift has a prequel called The Ultimate Life and a sequel called The Ultimate Legacy.)

"For the last two years, I have come from California to Clay Clark's Thrivetime Show conference/seminar, and I must say that I didn't know what to expect at first, but it's EXCEPTIONAL. If you are serious and I mean really serious about your career, your entrepreneurship and your wealth creation ability. I strongly, strongly implore you to come to Tulsa, invest the two days, it will change your life. It's quite extraordinary and I'm a tough grader."

MICHAEL LEVINE

(The publicist and public relations expert of choice for 58 Academy Award winners, 34 Grammy Award winners, and 43 New York Times best-sellers including Michael Jackson, Barbra Streisand, Prince, Nike and others.)

"He helped us to grow 4,000% from February to February! In the last two and a half days we have bettered our entire month of last year's February. The phone is blowing up. And everything is just blowing up! It's like a rocket ship and we are just pitching ourselves actually!"

JULIANA GRIMNES

(Co-Founder of www.GiveADerm.com)

"Clay Clark has been recognized nationally by the White House as Oklahoma's Small Business Entrepreneur of the Year. He has learned to leverage his business acumen and now finds himself in multiple successful business partnerships. This book extends his winning talks beyond sold-out conferences to an audience of thousands more nationwide and around the world. He will open up passageways for others to live beyond the "just surviving" mentality. He celebrates success wherever it is found. He understands the hard work and dedication required.

He really does admire Napoleon Hill and fills his life with Mr. Hill's actionable quotes. They are all through this book. As I look at Clay's success and his larger-than-life vision for his future, he is well on his way to emulating the man he so admires. And quite frankly, he is placing him in a similar position to be admired and quoted as his life and businesses continue to THRIVE. Oftentimes, people offering advice simply trust that the message is understood and move on, but not Clay Clark. He is committed to being in your face for your success.

Not afraid of repetitious conversation and in-your-face humor, he is committed to each reader getting the message. Embracing and implementing the action steps in his books and training. Clay Clark is obsessed with implementing the action steps around your "big idea." This man gets emotional over your business success – maximizing your talents and potential. He remembers his dorm-room start and fully celebrates yours. Quoting Clay, "My friend, as you can tell by now, running a successful business is about so much more than just having a 'big idea.'

Your BIG IDEA is important, but the overwhelming majority of what will make your business succeed or fail has little to do with the "big idea" itself and everything to do with the execution of the "big idea." Clay leaves us no doubt that action on our part matters. His life as well as his insightful consulting encounters become a clear window through which we can look and see what is possible in many of our lives if we are willing to put in the time and effort necessary to turn ideas into reality. Clay clearly points out that our "want to" becomes the driver of our actions or lack of actions.

Yes, I could have failed had I not embraced the notion that execution of a plan matters. Clay is right. His life challenges us to not settle, but to THRIVE. In doing so, we place ourselves in a position to light the darkness for others. It is in our reach to others that we truly maximize our existence on this planet. If I were still home in the Delta doing the same thing all those around me were doing, I seriously doubt if I would be able to light the pathway for myself or others. Today I am lighting the darkness as a businessman and writer, telling others what is possible for their lives. Clay's passionate plea for others to move beyond merely surviving comes from an honest place of caring. Why fail when you can THRIVE? Thank you, Clay, for not being afraid to step out beyond the ordinary and for inviting us along on your remarkable journey."

CLIFTON L. TAULBERT

(The first African American west of the Mississippi to found a bank, a Pulitzer-Prize Nominated and best-selling author, long-time Clay Clark mentor and the President of the Building Community Institute President & CEO)

"We definitely feel the growth. It's been amazing. Clay Clark has really helped us to expand. It was scary at first. I know I needed someone to guide us through this, through employees, through income, through spending. There are a lot of problems when you have a business and you can become very overwhelmed very fast. It's the best decision we've ever made!"

VIRGINIA MINGIONE, FNP-C
(NewConcept.Healthcare)

What Does the Phrase 'Elephant In The Room' Mean?

The metaphorical idiom "elephant in the room" refers to a **significant, obvious issue that people are avoiding or ignoring,** and it's likely rooted in a 19th-century Russian fable by Ivan Krylov, "The Inquisitive Man." The metaphorical elephant represents an obvious problem or difficult situation that people do not want to talk about.

» When someone has a bad haircut everyone notices it, but no one wants to talk about it.

» When you are in an elevator with four people and you smell a certain rectal-related smell and that smell is not coming from you, everyone notices it, but no one wants to talk about it.

» When a man/boss is sleeping with the employees they manage, everyone notices it, but no one wants to talk about it.

» When a man has ketchup on his face, or leaves his fly open, everyone notices it, but no one wants to talk about it.

» When a man is cheating on his wife with one of his employees and a pregnancy becomes more obvious, everyone notices it, but no one wants to talk about it.

» When just 1 out of 1,000 Americans will achieve financial success by default, everyone knows it, but no one wants to talk about it.

Let's get to work turning your dreams into reality!

....

"23 And whatsoever ye do, do it heartily, as to the Lord, and not unto men; 24 Knowing that of the Lord ye shall receive the reward of the inheritance: for ye serve the Lord Christ."

COLOSSIANS 3:23-24

Why Is Elephant In The Room Named "Elephant In The Room?"

I chose to name the men's grooming lounge Elephant In The Room, because I thought that it was a concept or premise that most great people like you could relate to and because I wanted to address two proverbial Elephants In The Room.

1st - I wanted to talk about the bad haircut experience that is all too common for most men. I believe that a haircut is not something that men should have to endure. I believe that our haircut should be a positive, affordable, and uplifting experience and not something that should take a nuclear half-life to receive.

2nd - I wanted to talk about entrepreneurship and how to become successful as an entrepreneur. I've been self-employed since I was 15 years old, working out of my parent's basement growing DJConnection.com into one of America's largest entertainment companies while simultaneously growing my graphic design and t-shirt printing business.

....

"I've learned that people will forget what you said, people will forget what you did, but people will never forget how you made them feel."

MAYA ANGELOU
(The iconic actress, poet and civil rights activist)

What Do You Get As An Elephant In The Room Member?

With our month-to-month memberships, you are essentially pre-purchasing your next Elephant In The Room Men's Grooming Lounge experience a haircut at a discount.

> » **You will receive a chance to win a dream vacation to Hawaii.**

> » **You will always be greeted by a friendly handshake and a kind smile.**

> » **You will receive a cold beverage.**

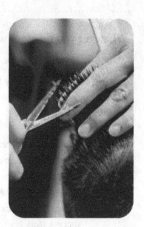

- » **You will receive a professional men's grooming consultation.**

- » **You will receive a relaxing shampoo and conditioner.**

- » **You will receive a scalp massage complete with essential oils.**

- » **You will receive a tailored haircut.**

- » **You will receive a nape shave.**

- » **You will receive professional styling.**

- » **You will receive access to unlimited clean-ups in between monthly appointments.**

- » **You will receive a free copy of this book.**

You will receive a ticket and access to the business growth and entrepreneurship workshops that I have been hosting since 2005 featuring past guests such as:

 » The legendary football player turned entrepreneur, Tim Tebow

 » The man who runs the Trump Organization, Eric Trump

 » The legendary best-selling author of the Rich Dad Poor Dad series Robert Kiyosaki

 » The man who turned around Harley-Davidson, Ken Schmidt

 » The legendary comedian, actor, and former Saturday Night Live cast member, Jim Breurer

Learn more at www.ThrivetimeShow.com

"Whatever you do, do it well. Do it so well that when people see you do it, they will want to come back and see you do it again, and they will want to bring others and show them how well you do what you do."

WALT DISNEY

(Walt began developing his skills as a cartoonist as a very young kid while living on a farm in Missouri. Walt did the voice for Mickey Mouse. Walt Disney won 22 Academy Awards and was nominated for an Academy Award 59 times. If you do your research, it could be argued that it took Walt Disney 4,015 nights to become an overnight success story.)

"Education is the key to unlock the golden door of freedom."

GEORGE WASHINGTON CARVER

(Despite being born into the horrors of slavery, George Washington Carver (1864 - 1943) was an American agricultural scientist and inventor who promoted alternative crops to cotton and methods to prevent soil depletion. He was one of the most prominent black scientists of the early 20th century. While a professor at Tuskegee Institute, Carver developed techniques to improve types of soils depleted by repeated plantings of cotton. He wanted poor farmers to grow other crops, such as peanuts and sweet potatoes, as a source of their own food and to improve their quality of life.)

What Is the Purpose of This Book?

I wrote this book for you because my desire is to provide you access to the business knowledge that took me nearly 30 years to acquire. I grew up poor and I was always searching for a mentor who could teach me how to become successful. As my father (may he rest in peace) was working at a furniture store, a gas station, delivering pizzas, going back to school, working the night shift and doing everything he could possibly do to put food on our table, I became both consciously and subconsciously obsessed about how to escape the rat race and how to become financially successful.

....

"The difference between great people and everyone else is that great people create their lives actively, while everyone else is created by their lives, passively waiting to see where life takes them next. The difference between the two is living fully and just existing."

MICHAEL GERBER

(A ThrivetimeShow.com Podcast guest, and the legendary best-selling author of The E-Myth book series)

Not knowing where to start, I started DJConnection.com out of my parent's basement while simultaneously starting a t-shirt and graphic design business. Because I didn't have mentors, I had to learn from my mistakes and from trial and error. Eventually I found books like Napoleon Hill's *Think & Grow Rich*, Dale Cale Carnegie's *How to Win Friends & Influence People*, John Maxwell's *21 Irrefutable Laws of Leadership*, Jerry Vass' *Soft Selling In a Hard World*, Robert Kiyosaki's *Rich Dad Poor Dad*. Soon I found myself working at Applebee's, Target and DirecTV while paying my way through Oral Roberts University and then Oklahoma State University. Quickly I discovered that whether I was attending St. Cloud State, Oral Roberts University or Oklahoma State University, the skills I needed to learn to become a successful entrepreneur and that business mindset and knowledge were not going to be taught at college. However, I was on a tireless quest to become my best and to learn how to become successful.

After 7 years of grinding and at the age of 22, I was recognized by the Tulsa Chamber of Commerce as the Young Entrepreneur of the Year for the success of DJConnection. com. For some reason this validation, the media buzz, and the awards generated opened my eyes to the importance of seeking mentorship from proven entrepreneurs. Including the Tulsa-based entrepreneur who helped to introduce the Stairmaster to the marketplace, Clifton Taulbert and the Tulsa-based self-made super success story, Doctor Robert Zoellner. However, it turns out that most super successful entrepreneurs have a lot of money and very little time.

....

"No one lives long enough to learn everything they need to learn starting from scratch. To be successful, we absolutely, positively have to find people who have already paid the price to learn the things that we need to learn to achieve our goals."

BRIAN TRACY

(The legendary best-selling author, speaker and business growth trainer)

Although I have previously written 30+ books in the past written for national and regional audiences, I am specifically writing this book for YOU as the founder of The Elephant In The Room Men's Grooming Lounge. I am writing this book for YOU and to address the Elephant In The Room that by just 1 out of 1,000 people will become financially successful by default. Consider this book to be my personal invitation to YOU to come and join us at our next in-person business growth workshop hosted right here in Tulsa, Oklahoma. I sincerely hope that I can meet you in person at one of our workshops, or that I randomly run into you one day at one of The Elephant In Room Men's Grooming Lounge shops.

Who Am I?

(Clay Clark, Founder of Elephant In The Room Men's Grooming Lounge)

I was the 2007 Oklahoma SBA Young Entrepreneur of the Year:

U.S. Small Business Administration

SBA
Your Small Business Resource

Oklahoma District Office
301 NW 6ᵗʰ Street, Suite 116 Oklahoma City, OK 73102   405/609-8000   (fax) 405/609-8990

February 21, 2007

Mr. Clayton Thomas Clark
DJ Connection Tulsa, Inc.
8900 South Lynn Lane Road
Broken Arrow, Oklahoma 74102

Dear Mr. Clark:

Congratulations! You have been selected as the **2007 Oklahoma SBA Young Entrepreneur of the Year.** On behalf of the U.S. Small Business Administration (SBA), I wish to express our appreciation for your support of small business and for your contributions to the economy of this State.

In recognition of your achievement, **an awards luncheon will be held Tuesday, May 22, 2007** at Rose State College in Midwest City, Okla. The luncheon is sponsored by the Oklahoma Small Business Development Center. Two complimentary luncheon tickets have been reserved for you and one guest.

Arrangements for the luncheon are still being finalized. You will be notified of the details as soon as they become available. You are encouraged to bring family, friends, and business associates. Upon presentation of your award, you will have the opportunity to make acceptance comments.

Also, for our awards brochure, please email an electronic photo of yourself to darla.booker@sba.gov by Friday, March 16.

Again, congratulations on your outstanding accomplishment.

Sincerely,

Dorothy (Dottie) A. Overal
Oklahoma District Director

I Live Entrepreneurship & I Teach It

I have founded/grown many successful businesses including (alphabetically speaking):

www.EITRLounge.com

www.EpicPhotos.com

www.MakeYourLifeEpic.com

www.MakeYourDogEpic.com

Tip Top K9 Franchising

Party Perfect Rentals

www.ThrivetimeShow.com

www.DJConnection.com

(I co-founded Tip Top K9 Franchising and helped the established brand of Tip Top K9 to grow from a single dog training business and location to over a dozen locations during my time with the brand.)

Real Clients, Real Results

Throughout my 20 years working as a business consultant I have helped thousands of REAL entrepreneurs to grow their REAL businesses including the many examples found throughout the pages of this book. To find their video testimonials visit: www.ThrivetimeShow.com/Testimonials/

What Is My Occupation?

I start, grow, and help to scale successful, sustainable, and profitable businesses. I also teach entrepreneurs how to start, grow, and scale successful businesses. See thousands of my documented client success stories and case studies today at: https://www.ThrivetimeShow.com/Testimonials/

What Is the Format of This Book?

I am writing this book for YOU in a way that is conducive to how most people on the planet learn. Most of us need to see visuals in order for the concept of "workflows" to make sense. Most of us need to see visual examples for words to jump off of the page and into our minds as practical and actionable information. I am filling this book with cartoons I have drawn over the years because (truth be known) I am a song-writing musician, a designer, and an artist. However, in order to fund the pursuit of my artistic endeavors I've chosen to start and grow successful businesses while helping thousands of entrepreneurs to become successful as well. When I write THOUSANDS, I do mean THOUSANDS and you can see their success stories at: www.ThrivetimeShow.com/Testimonials/

"Genius is one percent inspiration, ninety-nine percent perspiration."

THOMAS EDISON

(The man who is credited with being the founder of GE and the inventor of recorded audio, recorded video, the first modern light bulb and more)

It is often said that a picture is worth a thousand words. Well, if that is true, then perhaps this book will be worth 50,000 + words for you as I have filled this book with what I call CLAYMATIONS. These are drawings that are meant to supply you a profound knowledge bomb in an easily understandable way. However, to balance it out, I shall keep this book action-packed, and easily digestible because the legendary playwright, poet and actor William Shakespear once wrote, "Brevity is the soul of wit" and the legendary co-founder of Apple and the man who introduced the personal computer, the iPod, the iPhone and the iPad, once said, "Simplicity scales, complexity fails."

....

"If you want to go somewhere, it is best to find someone who has already been there."

ROBERT KIYOSAKI

(A multiple-time ThrivetimeShow.com podcast guest, an author who has co-written two books with America's 45th & 47th President Donald J. Trump, the legendary best-selling author of the Rich Dad Poor Dad book series, an investor, a podcaster and a man who has actually spoken live and in-person at our Thrivetime Show business growth conference in Tulsa, Oklahoma)

What Are the Best Ways to Connect?

- As an Elephant In The Room Men's Grooming Lounge member you can claim your complimentary tickets to our next 2-Day interactive business growth workshop at www.ThrivetimeShow.com. Or by texting me directly and (918) 851-0102.

- You can buy all 30+ books that I have written on Amazon.com, and you can download 100% of the books that I have written for free today at: www.ThrivetimeShow.com/free-resources/ .

- You can listen to my 6X iTunes chart-topping ThrivetimeShow.com business podcast on Spotify or iTunes featuring past guests such as:

8x *New York Times* Best-Selling Author and Leadership Expert, John Maxwell

 Celebrity Chef, Entrepreneur, and *New York Times* Best-Selling Author, Wolfgang Puck

 Legendary Former Key Apple Employee Turned Venture Capitalist, Best Selling Author, Guy Kawasaki

 New York Times Best-Selling Co-Author of Rich Dad Poor Dad, Sharon Lechter

 Senior pastor of the largest church in America with over 100,000 weekly attendees (Lifechurch.tv), Craig Groeschel

 One of America's most trusted financial experts and has written nine consecutive *New York Times* bestsellers with 7 million+ books in print, David Bach

 Legendary Conservative Strategist, Roger Stone

 NBA Hall of Famer, David Robinson (2-time NBA Champion, 2-time Gold Medal Winner)

 Senior Editor for *Forbes* and 3x Best-Selling Author, Zack O'Malley Greenburg

 Most Downloaded Business Podcaster of All-Time (EOFire.com), John Lee Dumas

 The 25th U.S. National Security Advisor and Retired U.S. Army General, General Michael Flynn

 New York Times Best-Selling Author of *Purple Cow*, and former Yahoo! Vice President of Marketing, Seth Godin

 Co-Founder of the 700+ Employee Advertising Company (AdRoll), Adam Berke

Emmy Award-winning Producer of the Today Show and *New York Times* Best-Selling Author of *Sh*tty Moms*, Mary Ann Zoellner

 New York Times Best-Selling Author of Contagious: Why Things Catch On and Wharton Business Professor, Jonah Berger

 New York Times Best-Selling Author of *Made to Stick* and Duke University Professor, Dan Heath

 International Best-Selling Author of *In Search of Excellence*, Tom Peters

 NBA Player and Coach, Muggsy Bogues (Shortest player to ever play in the league)

 NFL Running Back, Rashad Jennings (and Winner of Dancing with the Stars)

 Lee Cockerell (The former Executive Vice President of Walt Disney World who once managed 40,000 employees)

 Michael Levine (PR consultant of choice for Michael Jackson, Prince, Nike, Charlton Heston, Nancy Kerrigan, etc.)

 Billboard Contemporary Christian Top 40 Recording Artist, Colton Dixon

 Conservative Talk Pundit, Frequent Fox News Contributor, Political Commentator and Best-Selling Author, Ben Shapiro

Find thousands of additional guests at Thrivetimeshow.com

Introduction

Have you ever desired to grow a business, but you just felt stuck? Have you ever wanted to successfully grow a business and your income in a sustainable way that won't take over every waking second of your life? If you will invest the time needed to read the content found in this book you will learn:

» How to grow a successful business in a world where Inc. Magazine reports, "96% of Businesses Fail Within 10 Years." https://www.inc.com/bill-carmody/why-96-of-businesses-fail-within-10-years.html

» How to market your business in the hyper competitive cluttered world of commerce.

» How to generate high-quality leads from your ideal and likely buyers while gaining traction in this world filled with perpetual distraction.

» How to escape the rat race and the self-employment doom loop of building a job and not a business. JOB = Just Over Broke

» How to systemize every aspect of your business to reduce waste and expenses while increasing your capacity to grow and scale.

» How to hire, inspire, train, and retain top quality teammates and employees in a world where The U.S. Chamber of Commerce reports that "75% of employees steal from the workplace and that most do so repeatedly." https://www.cbsnews.com/news/employee-theft-are-you-blind-to-it/.

» How to design the repeatable processes, systems and workflows needed to grow.

» How to properly and profitably manage your cashflow so that financially and figuratively speaking you won't end up living in a van down by the river.

If you are looking to learn how to create time-freedom and financial-freedom creating business, you have come to the right place. However, although some business coaches, experts and authors don't need an introduction, I believe I do need an introduction because I am not famous, and because, in this world filled with charlatans and bogus experts, YOU will know that I actually know how to help YOU grow YOUR REAL business.

BEHOLD, THE PROVEN PATH TO SUCCESS

(1) ESTABLISH REVENUE GOALS

What are your yearly gross revenue goals?

_____

What are your total weekly gross revenue goals?

_____

(2) DETERMINE THE BREAK-EVEN NUMBERS

Number of customers/ sales to break even?

_____

(3) DEFINE WORK WEEK: NUMBER OF HOURS

How many hours are you willing to work?

_____

What are your boundaries?

_____

(6) CREATE 3-LEGGED MARKETING STOOL

Leg 1 _____

Leg 2 _____

Leg 3 _____

(5) IMPROVE BRANDING

On a scale of 1-10, with 10 being the highest, how highly would you rate your website, print pieces, and social media?

_____

(4) DEFINE YOUR UNIQUE VALUE PROPOSITION:

Who are your top 3 competitors?

_____

Have you mystery shopped your competitors?

_____

(7) CREATE A SALES CONVERSION SYSTEM

Sales scripts? _____

Recorded calls? _____

One sheets? _____

Pre-Written emails?_____

Lead trackers?_____

(8) DETERMINE SUSTAINABLE CUSTOMER ACQUISITION COSTS

What does it cost to obtain each customer?

_____

Do you have a tracking sheet? _____

Weekly advertising spend? _____

(9) CREATE REPEATABLE SYSTEMS, PROCESSES, AND FILE ORGANIZATION

What daily, core, repeatable, actionable processes are not documented into script or checklist form?_____

What processes and systems are not repeatable?

_____

Do you have checklists for all positions?

(12) CREATE HUMAN RESOURCES AND RECRUITMENT SYSTEMS

• Who are your A players? _____
• Who are your B players? _____
• Who are your C players? _____
• When is your weekly staff meeting? _____
• When is your weekly group interview? _____

(11) CREATE A SUSTAINABLE AND REPETITIVE WEEKLY SCHEDULE

When is your weekly group interview?_____

When is your daily group huddle?_____

(10) CREATE MANAGEMENT EXECUTION SYSTEMS

What people on your team will not do their jobs?

_____

Do you have merit-based pay installed? ____

(13) CREATE YOUR ACCOUNTING AND AUTOMATE THE EARNING OF MILLIONS

Are you using Clay Clark's Ultimate tracking sheet?_____

DETERMINE THE POINT OF ACHIEVING FINANCIAL SUCCESS?

(14) F7 GOALS

1-Faith _____

2-Family _____

3-Friendship _____

4-Fitness _____

5-Finances _____

6-Fun _____

7-Focus _____

27

> DAD, IF I GO OUT AND SPEND ALL OF MY TIME LOOKING FOR A JOB I MIGHT MISS AN EMPLOYER WHO IS TRYING TO CALL ME.

"ACTION IS THE REAL MEASURE OF INTELLIGENCE."
– NAPOLEON HILL
BEST-SELLING SUCCESS AUTHOR OF "THINK AND GROW RICH"

CHAPTER 1:

ACTION IS THE REAL MEASURE OF INTELLIGENCE

"In all labor there is profit, But
mere talk leads only to poverty."
Proverbs 14:23

As I write this book I am a 44-year-old man who is a father of 5 kids and the husband to an incredible wife, Vanessa Clark. We have been married for over 23 years and we are busy people just like you. Frankly I could say that I don't have the time needed to write this book. I host the daily www.ThrivetimeShow.com podcast, I own and operate several businesses, I run two hobby farms, I manage real estate investments, our business growth coaching program mentors 160 clients, I have an incredible dog named Davis, I have hundreds of fruit trees to tend to, chickens to feed and lots of figurative and literal weeds to pull. However, I have chosen to block out the time needed to write this book and you are choosing to block out time to read it. What's the point? The time will never be just right and you and I both must learn how to block out time for what matters most to us and it's a daily battle to find time to focus on what matters and what is going to help us achieve our goals. I believe every day that we have is a gift from God and what we choose to do with it is our gift to him. You may not agree, but I believe that God is calling all of us in the following 7 areas and more:

» **Faith: What are your faith goals?**
_____

» **Family: What are your family goals?**
_____

» **Finances: What are your financial goals?**
_____

» **Fitness: What are your fitness goals?**
_____

» **Friendship: What are your friendship goals?**
_____

» **Fun: What are your fun goals?**
_____

» **Focus: What are your focused time goals?**
_____

I remember the overwhelming thoughts I had when starting my first business DJConnection.com. I remember thinking about how I would earn the money needed to start my business. I remember doing the math in my college dorm room and determining that if I had three full-time jobs, I could earn enough money to start buying the copious amounts of speakers, sound and lighting equipment I would need to provide the entertainment services that I would render in route to building one of America's largest wedding and corporate entertainment companies. At the peak of that business and before I sold the business, we were doing 4,000 events per year, which is approximately 80 events every weekend. Think about the logistics, the vans, the equipment, the staffing, the lighting, the gear, the insurance, the sales, the marketing, the branding, the accounting that it takes to successfully deliver results and to WOW 4,000 customers per year to an average audience size of nearly 250 guests per event. Just thinking about the details can be overwhelming. However, eventually we just have to start. We have to start with the tools we have and the resources we have access to. We just have to start.

However, twelve years later after having grown dozens of companies, I remember being at ease mentally while starting Elephant In The Room Men's Grooming Lounge. I remember how great it felt knowing that I had a specific, linear and step-by-step plan in place that would work as long as I worked the plan. When I started Elephant In The Room Men's Grooming Lounge, I was supporting my wife, and our five kids while also supporting an adult who I did not give birth to, I remember doing the math and being confident that I knew exactly what needed to be done to grow the business because I had gained a full knowledge of the predictable process of starting and growing successful businesses.

I remember determining what it would cost me to build out our first location and I remember having laser-focused clarity on the specific plan that needed to be implemented to turn The Elephant In The Room Men's Grooming Lounge from an idea into reality.

In order for you and I to turn our big goals into reality we must become masters at setting S.M.A.R.T. goals that are Specific, Measurable, Actionable, Realistic & Time-Sensitive.

Want to Grow a Sustainably Successful Business?

» **Step 1 - Establish Your Revenue Goals**

» **Step 2 - Determine Your Break-Even Numbers**

» **Step 3 - Define the Number of Hours Per Week You Are Willing to Work**

» **Step 4 - Define Your Unique Value Proposition**

» **Step 5 - Improve Branding**

» **Step 6 - Create 3-Legged Marketing Stool & a Powerful No-Brainer**

» **Step 7 - Create a Sales Conversion System**

» **Step 8 - Determine Sustainable Customer Acquisition Costs**

» **Step 9 - Create Repeatable Systems, Processes & File Organization**

> » **Step 10 - Create Management Execution Systems**
>
> » **Step 11 - Create a Sustainable & Repetitive Weekly Schedule**
>
> » **Step 12 - Create Human Resources & Recruitment Systems**
>
> » **Step 13 - Create Accounting & Automate Earning Millions**
>
> » **Step 14 - Determine the Point of Achieving Financial Success**

....

"Begin with the end in mind."

STEPHEN COVEY

(The best-selling author of The 7 Habits of Highly Effective People)

Super Move #1 - Set Specific Goals

....

"If you want to be happy, set a goal that commands your thoughts, liberates your energy and inspires your hopes."

ANDREW CARNEGIE

(Andrew Carnegie was a Scottish-American industrialist and philanthropist. He grew up in poverty and began working 12 hours per day at the age of 13 earning $1.20 per week, which would be approximately $45 per week in today's economy (as of 2025). Carnegie led the expansion of the American steel industry in the late-19th century and became one of the richest Americans in history.)

A goal is not a goal if it is not specific. If something you desire is not specific, it is simply a wish or a hope. As an example, wanting to become financially successful is not a goal. However, an example of a specific goal would be to create an income stream of $100,000 per year by the year 2030 while working in the industry of selling pergolas, pools, hot tubs and outdoor living. A goal must be specifically defined, so that it can be acted upon and turned into reality.

Super Move #2 - Set Measurable Goals

....

"What gets measured gets improved."

PETER DRUCKER

(Peter Ferdinand Drucker was an Austrian American management consultant, educator, and author, whose writings contributed to the philosophical and practical foundations of modern management theory. He was also a leader in the development of management education, and invented the concepts known as management by objectives and self-control. Drucker developed an extensive consulting business built around his personal relationship with top management. He became legendary among many of post-war Japan's new business leaders trying to rebuild their war-torn homeland. He advised the heads of General Motors, Sears, General Electric, and IBM, among many others.)

As I was growing Elephant In The Room Men's Grooming Lounge and every other business that I have been involved with I am obsessed with measuring the results of our efforts. You and I must always remember to measure what we treasure because by default we will slack where we do not track.

Super Move #4 - Set Actionable Goals

....

"Successful people maintain a positive focus in life no matter what is going on around them. They stay focused on their past successes rather than their past failures, and on the next action steps they need to take to get them closer to the fulfillment of their goals rather than all the other distractions that life presents to them."

JACK CANFELD

(Jack Canfeld is the best-selling author and co-creator of the Chicken Soup for the Soul book series. The co-creator of the Chicken Soup for the Soul Series, Mark Victor Hansen has been interviewed on my ThrivetimeShow.com Business Podcast multiple times. The Chicken Soup for the Soul series has more than 250 titles and 500 million copies in print in over 40 languages.)

Although the rhythm of entrepreneurship is scary for most people, the pattern of success and the rhythm of entrepreneurship goes like this.

Step 1: Define the product and service that you believe the marketplace wants.

Step 2: Act based upon the facts you have gathered and the research you have conducted.

Step 3: Measure the results of your branding, marketing and the products/services you have delivered to the market place.

Step 4: Refine your business, products and services based upon the results that you are continuously tracking year and year, day after day.

Super Move #5 - Realistic

"Face reality as it is, not as it was or as you wish it to be."

JACK WELCH

(Jack Welch was the CEO who grew GE by 4,000% during his tenure by eliminating product lines that the marketplace did not want and that GE could not dominate, by removing C-Players from the workplace, by celebrating A-Players and B-Players in the workplace and by strictly and consistently measuring the results. Jack Welch was the best-selling author of the best-selling management book of all-time titled, Winning.)

Being realistic is not mean, it is just black or white, up or down, pass or fail, right or wrong. As examples:

» **It is not mean or negative if our big product and service ideas are being received well by the marketplace or not. The marketplace is either buying our product or service or it is not.**

» **It is not mean or negative that the score is kept during professional basketball games and that there is a winner or a loser of each game. A team either won the game or lost the game.**

» **It is not mean or negative that when objectively studying people you discover that one athlete can jump significantly higher than another athlete. A person either has the highest vertical leap or they do not.**

» It is not mean or negative to track sales percentages and key performance indicators in the workplace. A person is either having success in sales or they are not.

» It is not mean or negative when a member of the law enforcement community pulls someone over and gives them a speeding ticket for driving 30 miles over the speed limit. A person is either speeding or they are not.

» It is not mean or negative to remove an employee or business partner who has been married multiple times from the workplace and who has recently chosen to sleep with employees and to sleep with an employee while being married to someone else and while working as their direct supervisor and manager. A person can either be trusted or they cannot.

» It is not mean or negative if a customer points out the bathrooms need to be cleaned. The bathrooms were either cleaned or they weren't.

» It is not mean or negative for a manager to insist that all team members are on-time. A team member is either on time or they are late.

» It is not mean or negative that I grew up without financial resources. A person is either raised around wealth or they are not.

Super Move #6 - Set Time Sensitive Goals

"Discipline is the bridge between goals and accomplishment."

JIM ROHN

(Jim Rohn was an American entrepreneur, author, and motivational speaker. He wrote numerous books including How to obtain wealth and happiness. Rohn mentored Mark R. Hughes and life strategist Tony Robbins in the late 1970s. Others who credit Rohn for influencing their careers include authors/lecturers Mark Victor Hansen and Jack Canfield (Chicken Soup book series), Everton Edwards (Hallmark Innovators Conglomerate), Brian Tracy, Darren Hardy, and Harv Eker. Rohn coauthored the novel Twelve Pillars with Chris Widener.)

You and I must learn how to set time-sensitive goals with a sense of urgency. As an example, I woke up at three in the morning to write this book because I blocked out time in my schedule to do so and I want this book to be released by a certain date. If a deadline is not set, if a sense of urgency is not instilled we all have a tendency to drift in every area of our lives.

"A goal is a dream with a dead line."

NAPOLEON HILL

(The best-selling author of the Think & Grow Rich book series whom I named by son after. YES! I named my son Aubrey Napoleon-Hill Clark after Napoleon Hill, because the books written by Napoleon Hill changed my life. In fact, many years ago I was honored to be invited to be the keynote speaker at an event hosted in Charleston, South Carolina by the Napoleon Hill Foundation in conjunction with the Napoleon Hill Foundation and I've interviewed the best-selling author tasked with the resurrecting the unpublished writings of Napoleon Hill and the best-selling co-author of Rich Dad Poor Dad, Sharon Lechter.)

"Do not wait: the time will never be 'just right'. Start where you stand, and work whatever tools you may have at your command and better tools will be found as you go along."

- NAPOLEON HILL

(The best-selling author of the Think & Grow Rich book series whom I named by son after. YES! I named my son Aubrey Napoleon-Hill Clark after Napoleon Hill, because the books written by Napoleon Hill changed my life. In fact, many years ago I was honored to be invited to be the keynote speaker at an event hosted in Charleston, South Carolina by the Napoleon Hill Foundation in conjunction with the Napoleon Hill Foundation and I've interviewed the best-selling author tasked with the resurrecting the unpublished writings of Napoleon Hill and the best-selling co-author of Rich Dad Poor Dad, Sharon Lechter.)

"Life is not a dress rehearsal."

CLAY CLARK

(Alphabetically speaking: Clay Clark is the founder / co-founder of many successful brands including: DJConnection.com, EpicPhotos.com, EITRLounge.com, FearsClark.com Realty Group, MakeYourDogEpic.com, MakeYourLifeEpic.com, Party Perfect Rentals, The Tulsa Bridal Association Wedding Shows, ThrivetimeShow.com, TipTopK9.com Franchising (Clay Clark is not the founder of TipTopK9. com, however he is the man who teamed up with the founder to triple the revenue of the original location and to franchise the brand into 18 locations).

"What gets scheduled gets done."

LEE COCKERELL

(Lee Cockerell was a former Executive Vice President of Walt Disney World Resorts who once was responsible for managing 40,000 employees and 1,000,000 customers per week. Lee Cockerell has been featured on my ThrivetimeShow.com podcast numerous times and I helped Lee Cockerell to write and edit his book Time Management Magic: How to Get More Done Every Day and Move from Surviving to Thriving).

We must choose to be victims or victors.

We all make time for what is important to us. If your goals are real and you are serious about reaching them you will make time to clearly set specific, measureable, actionable, realistic and time sensitive goals. When you and I choose to take responsibility for our financial success it is possible. We must choose to become victors and to not be victims in the game of life. I personally grew up without money, stuttered as a kid, worked at Applebee's, Target & DirecTV in route to funding my first business DJConnection.com and have lived through the death of my best friend, and I had to watch my father slowly die from Lou Gehrig's Disease. However, I can tell you that success is possible if you are willing to diligently implement the principles being taught in this book.

....

"If you're going through hell, keep going."

WINSTON CHURCHILL

(The man who defiantly stood up and stood up alone against the Nazi Adolph Hitler as Hitler attempted to take over Europe and to remove God's people from the planet Earth.)

Want to Start or Grow a Successful Business?

If you have a burning desire inside you to start and grow a successful business, I would highly recommend that you would come and see us at one of our upcoming 2-Day interactive business growth workshops where we will teach you workflow design, marketing, branding, sales, organization chart mapping, pricing, online marketing, management, finance, best-practice human resources management systems and more. Remember, if YOU are an Elephant In The Room Men's Grooming Lounge member, YOUR access to our business growth workshops is included in your membership.

Learn More Today At: www.ThrivetimeShow.com

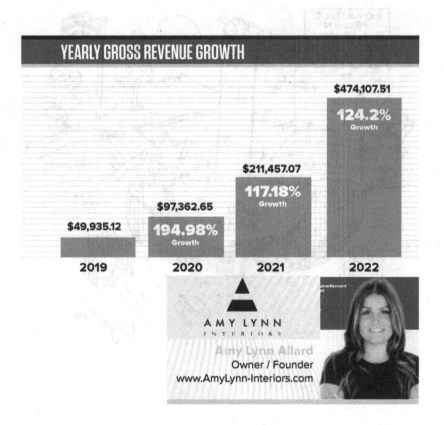

YEARLY GROSS REVENUE GROWTH

$49,935.12 — 2019

$97,362.65 — **194.98%** Growth — 2020

$211,457.07 — **117.18%** Growth — 2021

$474,107.51 — **124.2%** Growth — 2022

AMY LYNN
INTERIORS

Amy Lynn Allard
Owner / Founder
www.AmyLynn-Interiors.com

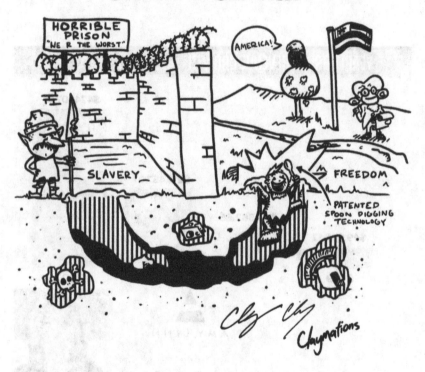

CHAPTER 2:

THE LEVEL OF YOUR PERSISTENCE & TENACITY WILL DETERMINE YOUR FINANCIAL CAPACITY

When starting and growing Elephant In The Room Men's Grooming Lounge I had to overcome challenges just like any small business. However, I do think that it is important to know and learn from the initial challenges that we faced while starting the business. Challenges included but not limited to:

» **While constructing our first location one of the contractors working on the job got severely injured.**

» **Very few Tulsa-based customers initially understood our business model and thus we had to beg my father, Thom Clark (may he rest in peace), Kirk Fryer (my long-time client and insurance agent), and every guy I had ever met to try out their first haircut for one dollar.**
Note: Kirk Fryer and Thom Clark (my dad) were the first two members. Literally 100% of our first haircut clients were consulting clients, my friends, or family.

> » **Some of the initial employees kept sleeping with each other despite the fact our rules and handbook clearly articulated this behavior was grounds for termination.**
>
> » **Most of our initial employees became our direct competitors.**
>
> » **We needed to create a memorable name and unique value proposition to stand out in the cluttered marketplace.**
>
> » **We had a neighbor nearby that was not fond of ever maintaining their landscaping thus early customers were often concerned about visiting our first location.**

However, regardless of how EPIC or non-EPIC the initial challenges that we faced may seem to you I know that you too have faced EPIC challenges and you are going to face EPIC challenges. In fact to quote Pastor Jackson Lahmeyer of Sheridan.Church, "Life looks like this. You are either in a storm, you are getting out of a storm or you are heading into a storm."

Thus, the advice that I would give to you specifically having interviewed some of the world's most successful people including: Wolfgang Puck, John Maxwell, NBA Hall of Fame Basketball Player, David Robinson, the co-founder of Netflix, Marc Randolph, the best-selling author of *Rich Dad Poor Dad*, Robert Kiyosaki, the co-founder of Square, Jim McKelvey and countless other success stories, you must decide that you will never quit and that when things get tough, you will persist until you achieve victory.

"Henceforth, I will consider each day's effort as but one blow of my blade against a mighty oak. The first blow may cause not a tremor in the wood, nor the second, nor the third. Each blow, of itself, may be trifling, and seem of no consequence. Yet from childish swipes the oak will eventually tumble. So it will be with my efforts today. I will be likened to the rain drop which washes away the mountain; the ant who devours a tiger; the star which brightens the earth; the slave who builds a pyramid. I will build my castle one brick at a time for I know that small attempts, repeated, will complete any undertaking.

I will persist until I succeed. I will never consider defeat and I will remove from my vocabulary such words and phrases as quit, cannot, unable, impossible, out of the question, improbable, failure, unworkable, hopeless, and retreat; for they are words of fools. I will avoid despair but if this disease of the mind should infect me then I will work on despite the despair. I will toil and I will endure. I will ignore the obstacles at my feet and keep my eyes on the goals above my head, for I know that where dry desert ends, green grass grows. I will persist until I succeed."

OG MANDINO

(The legendary self-help author and speaker of The Greatest Salesman In the World).

- What is the number one adversity facing you now?

  _____

  _____

- Write out why you will not let this temporary adversity and defeat stop you.

  _____

  _____

CHAPTER 3:

BUYING REAL ESTATE & GOLD ALLOWS YOU TO BUY WEALTH

The reason I was allowed to lease the commercial office space needed to start Elephant in the Room is because I developed the habit of saving money. You and I must choose to develop the habit of saving money to create opportunities in the future.

....

"Financial peace isn't the acquisition of stuff. It's learning to live on less than you make, so you can give money back and have money to invest. You can't win until you do this."

DAVE RAMSEY

(The legendary best-selling author, entrepreneur, podcaster, broadcaster and financial guru.)

I would sincerely encourage you to think about the following investment strategy which was taught to me by a man I know who owned a bank. I was taught this strategy when I was approximately 25 years old and it has never failed me. However, I am not giving you financial advice, I am just telling you the investment strategy that was taught to me and that works for me.

STEP 1 - Invest 25% of your income into real estate that is being sold by emotional people. A divorce is always a good source to find deeply discounted real estate. By the most beat up house a nice neighborhood. Look for tall grass and deferred maintenance in a high quality neighborhood and think about how much money you could bring in via monthly rent if you fixed up the property. Think about how much your monthly mortgage cost would be if you bought the property. Do the math and if you can buy a deeply discounted piece of real estate that you can rent out for much more than your monthly mortgage payment, then you should consider investing in that piece of real estate.

However, you must remember that the home you choose to live in typically does not generate revenue for you. Thus, your home is often not an asset, but rather it is a liability.

STEP 2 - Invest 25% of your income into the purchasing of gold. As the value of the U.S. dollar goes down in value due to inflation which is caused by government printing money that it does not have to pay for the purchasing of things it does not need, our hard-earned dollars will continue to decrease while the value of gold will continue to increase in value relative to the U.S. dollar. I have personally been investing in gold since 2005, when gold was nearly $444 per ounce. Today the price of gold is now at $3,084.70 per ounce (As of March 30th, 2025).

FUN FACTS:

In 1971, President Richard Nixon took America off of "The Gold Standard."

» **In 1975 the price of gold was $185 per ounce.**

» **In 1985 the price of gold was $327 per ounce.**

» **In 1995 the price of gold was $387 per ounce.**

» **In 2005 the price of gold was $444 per ounce.**

» **In 2015 the price of gold was $1,298 per ounce.**

» **In 2025 the price of gold was $3,084.70 per ounce (As of March 30th 2025)**

Want to learn more about how to buy gold?

Schedule a FREE consultation with my long-time friend and client, Andrew Sorchini at: www.BH-PM.com.

What Do America's Most Successful Entrepreneurs Have to Say About Gold?

The people listed below do not endorse Andrew Sorchini & Beverly Hills Precious Metals

"Since I was born in 1930 the dollar has depreciated by well over 90%."

WARREN BUFFET

(Investor and philanthropist who currently serves as the chairman and CEO of Berkshire Hathaway. Buffett's estimated net worth stood at US$149.6 billion, making him the seventh richest individual in the world.)

"People don't have adequate amounts of gold. When bad times come, gold is very effective...10-15% in the portfolio is worth giving thought to."

RAY DALIO

(American investor, hedge fund manager, and author who has served as co-chief investment officer of the world's largest hedge fund, Bridgewater Associates, since 1985. Bridgewater Associates, the hedge fund founded by Ray Dalio, had about $124 billion in assets under management.)

"Commodities such as gold and silver have a world market that transcends national borders, politics, religions, and race. A person may not like someone else's religion, but he'll accept his gold."

ROBERT KIYOSAKI

(Investor, podcaster, gold mine owner, and the legendary best-selling author of the Rich Dad Poor Dad series.)

"One thing that is a very important part of my portfolio all these years is gold. Gold hedges against inflation."

PATRICK BET-DAVID

(Patrick Bet-David is an Iranian-American businessman and podcaster. He is the host of the PBD Podcast and Valuetainment, which cover topics such as current events, business and pop culture, often featuring celebrity guests.)

STEP 3 - Keep 50% of your cash on hand for your next business plan.

» **What percentage of your disposable income will you invest in real estate?**

_____

» **What percentage of your disposable income will you invest in gold?**

_____

» **What percentage of your disposable income will you choose to keep on hand?**

_____

NOTE: I am honored, happy and glad to partner and work with my long-time friend and client Andrew Sorchini of Beverly Hills Precious Metals. If you want to schedule a free consultation with him visit www.BH-PM.com

"THE LOWER AN INDIVIDUAL'S ABILITY TO LEAD, THE LOWER
THE LID ON HIS POTENTIAL."
- JOHN MAXWELL

CHAPTER 4:

THE LOWER AN INDIVIDUAL'S ABILITY TO LEAD, THE LOWER THE LID ON HIS POTENTIAL

The office space was leased to me based on my reputation. The initial members visited our new shop because of my reputation as well.

There are no shortcuts even when dealing with haircuts. you and I must put in work and become known as hard working and diligent people who are faithful to our spouses, our clients, and our business partners.

We can't go through life cheating on our spouses, business partner, and clients, and expect to become respected leaders.

CHAPTER 5:

SAVE BEFORE YOU SPEND

....

"if it's important to you. Hire a coach. Amateurs don't have a coach. Professionals hire a coach."

ROBERT KIYOSAKI

(A multiple-time ThrivetimeShow.com podcast guest, an author who has co-written two books with America's 45th & 47th President Donald J. Trump, the legendary best-selling author of the Rich Dad Poor Dad book series, an investor, a podcaster and a man who has actually spoken live and in-person at our Thrivetime Show business growth conference in Tulsa, Oklahoma)

Becoming successful is a result of:

» Finding a problem that your ideal and likely buyers have

» Creating a solution that your ideal and likely buyers love

» Selling the solution for your
ideal and likely buyers

» Nailing and scaling the solution that you
are selling to your ideal and likely buyers

In order to build a scalable business model we must become coachable and teachable by people that know what they are talking about. Having worked with thousands of clients to help them to grow super successful businesses I can tell you the most coachable clients are always the most successful.

....

"I don't care how good you think you are, or how great others think you are—you can improve, and you will. Being relentless means demanding more of yourself than anyone else could ever demand of you, knowing that every time you stop, you can still do more. You must do more."

TIM GROVER

(The personal trainer for NBA legends:

Kobe Bryant - Kobe Bean Bryant was an American professional basketball player. A shooting guard, he spent his entire 20-year career with the Los Angeles Lakers in the National Basketball Association (NBA). Widely regarded as one of the sport's greatest and most influential players, Bryant won five NBA championships and was an 18-time All-Star, 4-time All-Star MVP, 15-time member of the All-NBA Team, 12-time member of the All-Defensive Team, the 2008 NBA Most Valuable Player (MVP), two-time NBA Finals MVP, and two-time scoring champion. He ranks fourth in league all-time regular season and postseason scoring. Bryant was posthumously voted into the Naismith Memorial Basketball Hall of Fame in 2020 and named to the NBA 75th Anniversary Team in 2021.

Michael Jordan - Michael Jeffrey Jordan was known by his initials MJ. He played 15 seasons in the National Basketball Association (NBA) between 1984 and 2003, winning six NBA championships with the

Chicago Bulls. He was integral in popularizing basketball and the NBA around the world in the 1980s and 1990s

Dwayne Wade - Dwyane Tyrone Wade Jr. is an American former professional basketball player who spent the majority of his 16-year career playing for the Miami Heat of the National Basketball Association (NBA) and won three NBA championships, was a 13-time NBA All-Star, an eight-time member of the All-NBA Team, and a three-time member of the All-Defensive Team.)

As an example, when I began helping Ryan and Rachel Wimpey to grow TipTopK9.com they were both very coachable. They were hard working and skilled dog training business owners and just needed to know the specific steps that they needed to take in order to turn their beloved business into a super success story and thriving business. In fact over the years, they had the following things to say about the mentorship I provided them:

....

"The search engine definitely helped. I wasn't implementing a DREAM 100. It doesn't matter how good you are if you aren't getting enough leads. Checklists for our bootcamps, processes, and structure and outlines for our private lessons, for our take home training, the sales script, and the call center scripts. Sitting down and line item by line item creating those scripts for the call center and sales was probably the biggest thing. It used to take me six months to do what we do in 6-8 weeks now. What we did with Clay, every week we come in and say this is what broke."

RYAN WIMPEY

(The Founder of TipTopK9.com)

What Did Ryan Wimpey and I First Work On to Grow TipTopK9.com?

"We did a logo first, got business cards, fliers, and then once you got the look we started making the website match the look. Autowrap and then all of our sales sheets, all of our fliers we got rid of the word documents. It doesn't matter how good you are at your craft if you don't have repeatable systems and they are not scripted out you are not going to succeed in replacing yourself. We tripled our income while growing to 17 locations. That was in 5 years. I could not have done that without hard systems."

How Did I Help to Grow TipTopK9.com?

"He's been working with so many different industries on systemizing every single part of them, that sometimes it takes a few times to hear something just like The Bible. It's really actionable information."

RYAN WIMPEY

(Founder of TipTopK9.com)

"They are just truly remarkable people. We love Clay, everything they have done for us. We would highly recommend them to anyone."

RYAN WIMPEY

(Founder of TipTopK9.com)

"We just want to give a huge thank you to Clay & Vanessa Clark. We worked with several different business coaches in the past and they were all about helping Ryan sell better, and just teaching sales, which is awesome, but Ryan is a really great salesman, so we didn't need that. We needed somebody to help us get everything that was in his head out into systems, into manuals and scripts and actually build a team. So now that we have systems in place we have gone from one location to ten locations in only a year."

RACHEL WIMPEY

(Founder of TipTopK9.com)

"They are so effective. If you don't use Clay and his team you are probably going to be pulling your hair out or you are going to be spending half of your time trying to figure out the online marketing game."

RYAN WIMPEY

(Founder of TipTopK9.com)

"We appreciate you and how far you have taken us. We have gone from 1 location to 10 locations in only a year. In Oct of 2016 we grossed $13K for the whole month, right now, it's 2018, the month of Oct, it's the 22nd, we've grossed $50K. We are just thankful for you, and your mentorship. We are really thankful that you guys have helped us to grow a business that we run now instead of the business running us. So thank you, thank you, thank you times one thousand!"

RYAN WIMPEY

(Founder of TipTopK9.com)

"He that walketh with wise men shall be wise: but a companion of fools shall be destroyed."

PROVERBS 13:20

(Found in the Bible and written by King Solomon, the wealthiest man in the history of Earth)

"When I was learning to become a dog trainer, we didn't learn anything about internet marketing or advertising at all. Clay has helped us make new logos, scripts for phones, scripts for emails, text messages. That's what is so great about working with Clay. They do it for us! They are so enthusiastic."

RYAN WIMPEY

(Founder of TipTopK9.com)

"My name is Rachel Wimpey. I've learned so much. I feel like my head is about to explode. Working on your business, instead of in your business because I have a tendency to just want to do it all myself. That's one thing that Clay really teaches is to have systems in place that you don't have to be there and your business can actually run without you. It's like an entrepreneur's playground. It's amazing here. It's really awesome. Clay's presentation and his style are just so different from most. It's been really one on one. He takes the time to answer your questions about your business, rather than just a generic answer. You implement those very same systems that he has discovered throughout all of the business he's run and it's just a lot of good information, really good presentation. If you don't come (to Clay Clark's business growth workshop) you are just going to be missing out on so much. Knowledge that is applicable. It's very hands-on. There is no upsell. Most business conferences are very, very expensive, this one is very affordable, it is definitely worth it. It will completely change your mindset. It will change your life. It's definitely worth it."

RACHEL WIMPEY

(Co-Owner of www.TipTopK9.com)

"I am Ryan Wimpey, I am originally from Tulsa, born and raised here. I definitely learned a lot about life design and making sure that the business serves you. The linear workflow for us and getting everything out and documented on paper is really important. We have workflows that are kind of all over the place so having a linear workflow and seeing that mapped out on multiple different boards is pretty awesome. That's pretty helpful for me."

RYAN WIMPEY

(Founder of TipTopK9.com)

"The atmosphere here is awesome. I definitely just stared at the walls figuring how to make my facility look like this place. This place rocks. It's invigorating, the walls are super...it's very cool. The atmosphere is cool. The people are nice. Very good learning atmosphere. I literally want to model it and steal everything that is here (at Clay Clark's office) at this facility and just create it just on our business side."

RYAN WIMPEY

(Founder of TipTopK9.com)

"Clay is hilarious. I literally laughed so hard that I started crying yesterday. The content is awesome off the charts! It's very interactive and you can raise your hand. The wizard teaches, but the wizard interacts and he takes questions and that is awesome. If you are not attending the conference you are missing three quarters to half of your life! You are missing the thought process. Just getting in the thought process of Clay Clark to me, just that is priceless. That's money!"

RYAN WIMPEY

(Founder of TipTopK9.com)

"There are no upsells or anything. The cost of this conference is quite a bit cheaper than business college. I went to a small private liberal arts college and got a degree in business and I didn't learn anything like they are teaching here. I didn't learn linear workflows, I learned stuff that I'm not using and I haven't been using for the last 9 years. So what they are teaching here is actually way better than what I got at business school and I went to what was actually ranked as a very good business school. The information that you are going to get is just VERY VERY beneficial and the mindset that you are going to get."

RYAN WIMPEY

(Founder of TipTopK9.com)

"Clay really helped us with his systems, taking us to the point of having ten or more employees, or doubling our size, helped us double our incomes."

RYAN WIMPEY

(Founder of TipTopK9.com)

"A wise man will hear, and will increase learning; and a man of understanding shall attain unto wise counsel."

PROVERBS 1:5

(Found in the Bible and written by King Solomon, the wealthiest man in the history of Earth)

Read the Original Full Story of How Clay
Clark Mentored & Helped Ryan Wimpey
to Grow & Scale TipTopK9.com HERE:

**https://www.justtulsa.com/business-
coach-tulsa-thrivetime/4/**

"In this next session, I got to sit in while Clay met with a client who specializes in custom vehicle wrapping (like a vinyl wrap that gets put on over the paint on your car, ya know?)

This was another name that I was familiar with, so it was pretty cool to meet the man in charge.

This meeting was heavily themed around tracking results for some different keywords that the Thrivetime business coaching program was helping this client to rank for.

Like the others, this meeting ended up with some performance tweaks to be made to the client's website that will nearly guarantee the client's business to show up higher for the keywords that he wants to show up for in Google.

Ryan Wimpey of www.TipTopK9.com Shares What He Learned At Clay Clark's Thrivetime Show Conference

The Tip Top K9 Dog Training Interview & TipTopK9.com Growth Story

At the conclusion of the aforementioned meeting, we step out of The Box That Rocks and Clay begins and starts his next meeting. Between the meetings, we get a brief chance to discuss the prior meeting's action points and the "how's" and "why's" of how those apply to growing a business into the best version of itself.

At this point, a couple in yellow shirts come in. They're from a company that has gone through a tremendous amount of growth since starting to work with Clay and the crew: Tip Top K9.

Clay offered to let me bounce a few questions off of them

after the meeting. Once they finished up, Tip Top K9 founder Ryan Wimpey came over to where I was waiting so I recorded a few questions that I asked him."

I'm going to transcribe this conversation to text, so I'll keep it fairly abbreviated for the sake of our collective sanity.

Tyler (Just Tulsa): So, the first time I had ever heard of Tip Top K9 was back around September in one of the Thrivetime business conferences. How long have you all been working with the Thrivetime business coaching program?

Ryan Wimpey of TipTopK9.com Dog Training: We've been working with them for 14 months or so now... Just a little bit over a year.

Tyler: And how did you all get hooked up with them?

Ryan Wimpey of TipTopK9.com Dog Training: I heard about the Thrivetime business coaching program when I heard Clay on a podcast called the Profit First Podcast. I was like, "Aw, this is good!", then I was like "Wait, this guy is from Tulsa?"

Watch Clay Clark's Interviews With Profit First Podcast Founder, Mike Mikalowitz:

Tyler: How has your business changed since you first started working with Clay?

Ryan Wimpey of TipTopK9.com Dog Training: It's definitely gotten a lot better. We've got a lot of systems and marketing in place now. I don't even worry about marketing anymore.

Tyler: So, does Thrivetime business coaching program handle that or do they just kind of get you all set up and let you all handle it from there?

Ryan Wimpey of TipTopK9.com Dog Training: Nope — they handle all of our marketing.

Tyler: Really?

Ryan Wimpey of TipTopK9.com Dog Training: Yeah. They do our YouTube ads, Facebook ads, re-targeting, and Google AdWords.

Tyler: And you feel like those marketing channels bring in a worthwhile amount of leads or business?

Ryan Wimpey of TipTopK9.com Dog Training: Oh yes — last week was actually our biggest week in terms of leads, ever.

Tyler: Of those marketing channels that you guys use to get in front of your ideal customers, what does your "Three-Legged Marketing Stool" consist of? (Note: this "three-legged marketing stool refers to an approach that Clay and Dr. Zoellner teach to make sure the high quality leads come in and sustainably keep doing so.)

Ryan Wimpey of TipTopK9.com Dog Training: Ours consists of our "Dream 100", search engine optimization, and AdWords.

[At this point, me and Ryan chat for a few minutes about how inexpensive pay-per-click advertising is between Google and social media these days.]

Ryan Wimpey of TipTopK9.com Dog Training: YouTube is working wonders for us right now. They made a great video for us.

Tyler: And when that gets in front of a prospect who has been to your website before (Note: aka re-targeting/re-marketing), you're only showing your ad to people that are likely to be interested in dog training in Tulsa to begin with, right?

Ryan Wimpey of TipTopK9.com: Exactly.

Tyler: During the last conference that I went to, Clay mentioned that you all were in the beginning phases of franchising out the Tip Top K9 model to some people in Idaho. Can you elaborate on that a little bit, please?

Ryan Wimpey of TipTopK9.com: We actually have a location in Owasso that just opened this week and we've got a location in Twin Falls, Idaho. We've got another location opening in Boise, Idaho in about 3 months.

TipTopK9 Dog Training Franchisee Brett Denton Shares How Implementing Clay Clark's Turn-Key Business Systems Has Helped Him to Grow & Scale Multiple Successful Businesses.

Tyler: Wow. That's gotta be insane to see a business that you started — the uniforms, the van, everything — being used by someone in a completely different state.

Ryan Wimpey of TipTopK9.com Dog Training: It is! Right now, we have 9 other trainers and 2 admin people, so looking back, it's crazy to think about how at one point I was doing the whole thing by myself out of a van.

Tyler: That's crazy...

Ryan Wimpey of TipTopK9.com Dog Training: I know — Clay really helped us with his systems, because — while we could get to 4 or 5 people — taking us to the point of having ten or more employees, or doubling our size, helped us double our incomes.

[At this point, me and Ryan start talking about our mutual adoration for the book The E-Myth Revisited. I won't bore you with the details of that little tangent.]

Tyler: How was working with the Thrivetime business coaching program key in bringing you all to the point of where you are now launching multiple franchise operations?

Ryan Wimpey of TipTopK9.com Dog Training: If I never had been able to step out of the day-to-day grind, I would've never had time to build the systems that have let us replace ourselves (referring to him and his wife, Rachel). So, she was able to work on the management systems and call center stuff, and I was able to train the trainers and come up with systems for private lessons and everything else. We were really able to pull back on our involvement because we were able to systemize everything. We don't have to worry about our marketing or our website. And when we have a coach who we have to stay accountable to on a weekly basis... It helps tremendously.

Tyler: Well, I'll let you all get back to working on your business! Thanks for your time!

Ryan Wimpey of TipTopK9.com Dog Training: Thanks!

» In what area of your life do you feel the most stuck? _____
_____

» What mentors can you seek out to help you get unstuck in this area? ___
_____

"It's better to hang out with people better than you. Pick out associates whose behavior is better than yours and you'll drift in that direction."

WARREN BUFFET

(Warren Edward Buffett is an American investor and philanthropist who currently serves as the chairman and CEO of Berkshire Hathaway. As a result of his investment success, Buffett is one of the best-known investors in the world. According to Forbes, as of 17 February 2025, Buffett's estimated net worth stood at US$149.6 billion, making him the seventh richest individual in the world. Berkshire Hathaway controls the following brands GEICO, Fruit of the Loom, See's Candies, Clayton Homes, Dairy Queen, Duracell, Benjamin Moore, BNSF, etc.)

To see thousands of REAL success stories
from REAL entrepreneurs check out:

**www.ThrivetimeShow.com and click
on the "Testimonials" button.**

"WHEN IT COMES TO INVESTING, SIMPLY ATTEMPT TO BE FEARFUL WHEN OTHERS ARE GREEDY, AND BE GREEDY WHEN OTHERS ARE FEARFUL."
- WARREN BUFFET

CHAPTER 6:

BE GREEDY WHEN THE MARKET IS FEARFUL, BE FEARFUL WHEN THE MARKET IS GREEDY

If you show up early, and obsess about wowing your customers, your boss, or whomever is paying you, then you will eventually increase your earnings. As you begin to earn more, it is very important that you invest and save your money wisely. Thus, I would encourage you to memorize the Warren Buffett quote pictured in the cartoon I created above. When the market is crashing and the value of real estate hits the bottom, that is a good time to buy and invest in real estate if you are buying high quality real estate in a nice part of your community. However, the worst time to buy real estate is when the market is booming and when real estate values have hit an all-time high. Remember, my friend, when investing in real estate. Buy low and sell high.

....

"Buy the dips."

ERIC TRUMP

(A long-time friend of Clay Clark, a frequent Thrivetime Show podcast guest who has appeared in person at Clay Clark's 2-day interactive business growth conferences held in Tulsa, Oklahoma. Eric Trump is the third child and second son of the president of the United States Donald Trump and his first wife Ivana Trump. Eric Trump is a trustee and executive vice president of his father's business, the Trump Organization, running it alongside his older brother Donald Jr. He also served as a boardroom judge on his father's television series The Apprentice.)

"Real estate cannot be lost or stolen, nor can it be carried away. Purchased with common sense, paid for in full, and managed with reasonable care, it is about the safest investment in the world."

FRANKLIN D. ROOSEVELT

(Also known as FDR, was the 32nd president of the United States, serving from 1933 until his death in 1945.)

"Ninety percent of all millionaires become so through owning real estate. More money has been made in real estate than in all industrial investments combined. The wise young man or wage earner of today invests his money in real estate."

ANDREW CARNEGIE

(Billionaire industrialist)

"Don't wait to buy real estate. Buy real estate and wait."

WILL ROGERS

(A legendary American vaudeville performer, actor, and humorous social commentator.)

"Buying real estate is not only the best way, the quickest way, the safest way, but the only way to become wealthy."

MARSHALL FIELD

(An American entrepreneur and the founder of Marshall Field and Company, the Chicago-based department stores. His business was renowned for its then-exceptional level of quality and customer service.)

- What is a set percentage of your income that you will choose to invest? _____

- What assets do you feel most comfortable with investing in? _____

"IF YOU WANT TO SAVE YOURSELF A BUNCH OF TIME, IT IS ALWAYS EASIER TO BE A PIRATE THAN A PIONEER."
– CLAY CLARK

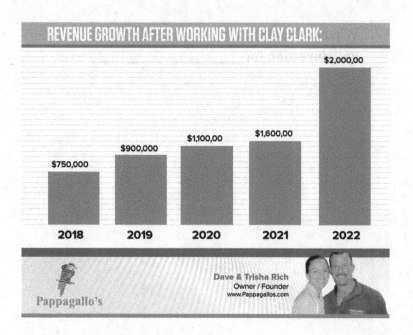

CHAPTER 7:

BE A PIRATE & NOT A PIONEER

When you are starting and growing a business you will run out of capital long before you reinvent the wheel. Thus, as shocking as it sounds, as I began researching the men's grooming industry, I quickly discovered that we were not the only people in the history of America, Oklahoma, or Tulsa to think of the concept of creating a Tulsa-based men's grooming experience, tailored haircuts, or a membership-based men's grooming business.

....

"Ideas are easy. Implementation is hard."

 GUY KAWASAKI

(A multiple-time ThrivetimeShow.com podcast guest, a best-selling author, a Silicon Valley venture capitalist, and one of the Apple employees originally responsible for marketing their Macintosh computer line in 1984.)

Thus, in order to truly understand the men's grooming industry, and to discover what the best and worst in the men's grooming industry were doing I decided to get my haircut at some of the highest rated grooming businesses in the following cities and more:

» **Austin, Texas**

» **Charlotte, North Carolina**

» **Chicago, Illinois**

» **Dallas, Texas**

» **Los Angeles, California**

» **New Orleans, Louisiana**

» **New York, New York**

» **San Diego, California**

To help discover the industries best decor, pricing, service, staffing and the overall business that would become The Elephant In The Room Men's Grooming Lounge, I traveled across the country in search of the best men's grooming businesses and experiences. As I traveled, I often met the founders of these local businesses and what I found was they all shared the following world-views and more.

» **They all firmly believed in the power of a first impression and in the importance of providing their customers with a quality men's grooming experience.**

» **They had a passion for men's grooming.**

» **They had a passion for providing quality beard grooming.**

» **They all prided themselves on offering the men in their city a unique, different and quality men's grooming experience.**

» **They all strived to set a standard of excellence in the men's grooming industry in their local market.**

» **They all worked hard.**

» **Unfortunately, most of them were struggling to survive financially.**

"Most entrepreneurs are merely technicians with an entrepreneurial seizure. Most entrepreneurs fail because you are working IN your business rather than ON your business."

MICHAEL GERBER

(A ThrivetimeShow.com Podcast guest, and the legendary best-selling author of The E-Myth book series)

Why would businesses owners with passion, dedication, next-level skills and an obsession for men's grooming be struggling financially? Most of these entrepreneurs were struggling financially because they were working in a business, but they did not know how to work on a business. These great people knew how to cut hair, but they did not know how to grow a successful business. Many of these entrepreneurs were in desperate need of a mentor who could provide them with the 3 C's of Mentorship:

- **Coaching** - Every aspiring entrepreneur needs to know the proven best-practice systems and processes needed to both start and grow a successful business.

- **Connections** - Every aspiring entrepreneur needs to know the right people. They need to have someone in their life that can introduce them to banks, initial customers, investors, potential customers, media outlets, vendors, contractors and more

- **Capital** - Every entrepreneur needs access to capital to both start and grow a successful business. Most of us don't have the ability to move in with family while we get our financial lives together. Most of us don't have access to a wealthy brother-in-law willing to invest in our ideas. Most of us don't have a sister willing to cover living expenses so we can use 100% of our income to invest in our business idea. Lastly, most of us don't have family willing to sign a lease for us.

....

"I have learned from both my own successes and failures and those of many others that it's the boring stuff that matters the most. Startup success is not a consequence of good genes or being in the right place at the right time."

ERIC REIS

(An American entrepreneur, blogger, and author of best-selling The Lean Startup, a book on the lean startup movement. He is also the author of The Startup Way, a book on modern entrepreneurial management.)

Many times aspiring entrepreneurs forget the need for proven mentors who can provide them with the 3 C's of Mentorship:

- » **Coaching**
- » **Connections**
- » **Capital**

The wisdom required to become a coach is something that can only be gained through diligently studying successful entrepreneurs, case studies, working with real businesses, and building real businesses. Connections are something that take a decade or more to develop. Capital is something that is difficult to come by if you have not developed the habit of saving.

Many times I have observed people get frustrated that they find themselves living with their extended family, divorced, and without capital, connections, and barely just getting by. Oftentimes I notice that the people that feel stuck in life cannot seem to see the correlation between their actions, their habits, their relationship failures, and their financial failures.

Again, In order to get unstuck I would argue that we all need access to:

- » **Coaching**
- » **Connections**
- » **Capital**

"Drifting, without aim or purpose, is the first cause of failure."

NAPOLEON HILL

(The best-selling author of the Think & Grow Rich book series whom I named by son after. YES! I named my son Aubrey Napoleon-Hill Clark after Napoleon Hill, because the books written by Napoleon Hill changed my life. In fact, many years ago I was honored to be invited to be the keynote speaker at an event hosted in Charleston, South Carolina by the Napoleon Hill Foundation in conjunction with the Napoleon Hill Foundation and I've interviewed the best-selling author tasked with the resurrecting the unpublished writings of Napoleon Hill and the best-selling co-author of Rich Dad Poor Dad, Sharon Lechter.)

If you are reading this book and you feel stuck, and you are in need of coaching, connections and capital, I would highly recommend that you attend one of our in-person two-day interactive business growth workshops. As an Elephant In The Room Men's Grooming Lounge member you can claim your complimentary tickets to our next 2-Day interactive business growth workshop at www.ThrivetimeShow.com.

"Professionals hire coaches, amateurs do not."

ROBERT KIYOSAKI

(A multiple-time ThrivetimeShow.com podcast guest, an author who has co-written two books with America's 45th & 47th President Donald J. Trump, the legendary best-selling author of the Rich Dad Poor Dad book series, an investor, a podcaster and a man who has actually spoken live and in-person at our Thrivetime Show business growth conference in Tulsa, Oklahoma)

"IF YOU WANT TO SAVE YOURSELF A BUNCH OF TIME, IT IS ALWAYS EASIER TO BE A PIRATE THAN A PIONEER."
- CLAY CLARK

CHAPTER 8:

KNOW YOUR NUMBERS OR YOU WILL GET POOR QUICK

Accounting, bookkeeping and knowing your numbers are not the kinds of topics that generally get most entrepreneurs excited, but they are the topics that you need to know and master if you are going to grow a successful business. As a business owner you simply must know the following numbers on a daily basis.

....

"Don't ever let your business get ahead of the financial side of your business. Accounting, accounting, accounting. Know your numbers."

TILMAN JOSEPH FERTITTA

(An American businessman and television personality. He is the chairman, CEO, and owner of Landry's, Inc. He also owns the National Basketball Association (NBA)'s Houston Rockets. Fertitta has been the chairman of the board of regents of the University of Houston System since 2009. As of February 2025, his net worth was estimated at $10.8 billion. He was placed at No. 99 on the Forbes 400 list. Forbes calls him the "World's Richest Restaurateur.")

You must know the metrics related to the revenue producing activities in your business.

Think about the business that you are growing and that you want to grow.

What are the core repeatable actionable processes that you must deliver on every day to make your business grow?

_____

_____

_____

_____

_____

What are those repeatable action steps that have to be knocked out on a daily basis to make your business boom?

_____

_____

_____

_____

_____

It is very important that you invest the time needed to create checklists, systems and processes for both accuracy and accountability. If you are going to build a successful organization you must be organized.

_____

_____

_____

_____

"We don't like checklists. They can be painstaking. They're not much fun. But I don't think the issue here is mere laziness. There's something deeper, more visceral going on when people walk away not only from saving lives but from making money. It somehow feels beneath us to use a checklist, an embarrassment. It runs counter to deeply held beliefs about how the truly great among us—those we aspire to be—handle situations of high stakes and complexity. The truly great are daring. They improvise. They do not have protocols and checklists. Maybe our idea of heroism needs updating."

ATUL GAWANDE

(The legendary Harvard professor, surgeon and best-selling author of The Checklist Manifesto: How to Get Things Right)

"BE LIKE A POSTAGE STAMP.
STICK TO IT UNTIL YOU GET THERE."
-HARVEY MACKAY

DETER MEND
MEDIOCRITY PL.
NOWHERE, UTAH

CLAY CLARK
777 SUCCESS AVE.
74119 TULSA, OK

Claymations

CHAPTER 9:

BE LIKE A POSTAGE STAMP, STICK TO IT UNTIL YOU GET THERE

When the excitement of the new car, the new girlfriend, the new wife, and the new business wears off it comes down to diligence, faithfulness and commitment. How can you maintain consistency on a daily basis? As an example, my ThrivetimeShow.com podcast has been number one on the iTunes charts 6 times. However, as I have now recorded well over 5,000 shows, it is abundantly clear to all of our listeners that more often than not I am not the most listened to podcast on the planet Earth. Think about it for a second. I have personally recorded and produced over 5,000 podcasts, yet I have only hit number one on the iTunes charts 6 times.

Is the fact above encouraging or discouraging?

"People around you, constantly under the pull of their emotions, change their ideas by the day or by the hour, depending on their mood. You must never assume that what people say or do in a particular moment is a statement of their permanent desires."

ROBERT GREENE, MASTERY

(A guest on the ThrivetimeShow.com podcast, an iconic author on strategy and power. When reading Robert Greene's books it is important to know that people that do not read the Bible and who do not adhere to God's laws often use The 48 Laws of Power against you in a nefarious way. I believe that it's important to know the moves that nefarious people will use against you so that you can protect yourself against the evil moves and the problems they will cause you. He has written seven international bestsellers, including The 48 Laws of Power, The Art of Seduction, The 33 Strategies of War, The 50th Law (with rapper 50 Cent), Mastery, The Laws of Human Nature, and The Daily Laws.)

Over the years, I have interviewed some of the biggest names and success stories in American business, yet think about how many big time guests have told me "NO" when I asked them to appear on my podcast. In fact, let me tell you a secret. Most of the people that I have invited to be a guest on my show have told me "NO." But, you know what I do? I just act like a postage stamp and I stick to it until I get there.

You Can Learn from Mentors Or Mistakes

However, to save you years of research, rejection and painful trial and error I have interviewed the following guests below (and more) and I have archived all of these interviews and more at ThrivetimeShow.com so that you can now learn from the following people and more:

FUBU Founder & ABC's Shark Tank Investor, **Daymond John**

 Billionaire Paychex Founder, **Tom Golisano**

 Billionaire Square Co-Founder, **Jim McKelvey**

 Senior Editor for *Forbes* and 3x Best-Selling Author, **Zack O'Malley Greenburg**

 Wired Magazine Co-Founder, Multiple-Time *New York Times* best-selling author, **Kevin Kelly**

 Legendary Best-Selling Author and Educator, **Robert Kiyosaki**

 Prolific Hit Song-Writer for Justin Bieber, Maroon 5, Gwen Stefani, Charlie Puth, Michael Buble, Jason Derulo, James Taylor, and **Ross Golan**

 Former President and Co-Founder of the Ritz-Carlton Hotel Company, **Horst Schulze**

 Former CEO of YUM! (A&W Restaurants, Taco Bell, Pizza Hut, KFC). During Novak's Tenure at Yum! Brands, the Company Doubled the Number of Restaurants to 41,000, Market Capitalization Grew to Almost $32 Billion from Just Under $4 Billion And It Was an Industry Leader In Return On Invested Capital, **David Novak**

 Harvard Business School Professor and Best-Selling Author, **Clayton Christensen**

 Iconic Neurosurgeon, Academic Author and the 17th United States Secretary of Housing and Urban Development, **Ben Carson**

Best-Selling Author of *The Carnivore Diet* and Doctor,
Shawn Baker ,MD

The Best-Selling Author of *The Subtle of Not Giving a _____*,
Mark Manson

The International Best-Selling Author of *The 48 Laws of Power*, the
50th Law, Mastery, The Laws of Human Nature, **Robert Greene**

The Best-Selling Author of the Iconic *E-Myth* Book Series,
Michael Gerber

The Blind Best-Selling Author & Emmy Award Winning
Filmmaker, **Jim Stovall**

NBA Player, Best-Selling Author and Entrepreneur,
Jonathan Isaac

The 13th Administrator of the (NASA) National Aeronautics and
Space and Oklahoma Congressman, **Jim Bridenstine**

Behance Founder and Vice President of Products at Adobe,
Scott Belsky

Honest Tea Founder, **Seth Goldman**

Former Adidas Executive that introduced Kanye West's Yeezy
Brand, **Eric Liedtke**

The Iceman, the Dutch Motivational Speaker, Guinness World
Record for Swimming Under Ice and Prolonged Full-Body Contact
with Ice, and He Holds a Record for a Barefoot Half-Marathon on
Ice and Snow, **Wim Hof**

8x *New York Times* Best-Selling Author and Leadership Expert,
John Maxwell

The Best-Selling Author of *Atomic Habits*,
James Clear

Iconic Comedian, Actress & Writer,
Roseanne Bar

Former Saturday Night Live Cast Member, Actor & Standup
Comedian, **Jim Breuer**

Celebrity Chef, Entrepreneur, and *New York Times* Best-Selling
Author, **Wolfgang Puck**

Legendary Former Key Apple Employee Turned Venture Capitalist,
Best Selling Author, **Guy Kawasaki**

Executive Vice President of The Trump Organization,
Eric Trump

New York Times Best-Selling Co-Author of *Rich Dad Poor Dad*,
Sharon Lechter

Senior Pastor of the Largest church in America With Over 100,000
Weekly Attendees (Lifechurch.tv),
Craig Groeschel

One of America's Most Trusted Financial Experts who has Written
Nine Consecutive *New York Times* Bestsellers with 7 Million+ Books
in print, **David Bach**

NBA Hall of Famer, **David Robinson** (2-time NBA
Champion, 2-time Gold Medal Winner)

Most Downloaded Business Podcaster of All-Time
(EOFire.com), **John Lee Dumas**

New York Times Best-Selling Author of *Purple Cow*, and Former
Yahoo! Vice President of Marketing, **Seth Godin**

Co-Founder of the 700+ Employee Advertising Company (AdRoll), **Adam Berke**

Emmy Award-winning Producer of the Today Show and *New York Times* Best-Selling Author of *Sh*tty Moms*, **Mary Ann Zoellner**

New York Times Best-Selling Author of *Contagious: Why Things Catch On* and *Wharton Business* Professor, **Jonah Berger**

New York Times Best-Selling Author of *Made to Stick* and *Duke University* Professor, **Dan Heath**

International Best-Selling Author of *In Search of Excellence*, **Tom Peters**

NBA Player and Coach, **Muggsy Bogues** (shortest player to ever play in the league)

NFL Running Back, **Rashad Jennings** (and Winner of Dancing with the Stars)

The Former Executive Vice President of Walt Disney World Who Once Managed 40,000 Employees, **Lee Cockerell**

PR Consultant of Choice for Michael Jackson, Prince, Nike, Charlton Heston, Nancy Kerrigan, etc., **Michael Levine**

Billboard Contemporary Christian Top 40 Recording Artist, **Colton Dixon**

Conservative Talk Pundit, Frequent Fox News Contributor, Political Commentator and Best-Selling Author, **Ben Shapiro**

MIT Graduate and Physicist Who Worked with James Cameron and Arnold Schwarzenegger on Documentaries Starring Matt Damon, Jessica Alba, Don Cheadle, America Ferrera Jack Black, Sigourney Weaver, Thomas Friedman, Olivia Munn, David Letterman, Gisele Bündchen, Joshua Jackson, and Harrison Ford. *Rolling Stone* has Called Him One of the "100 People Who Are Changing America,"

Joseph J. Romm

 Former NBA Player, Turned NBA Coach, **Phil Pressey**

 Former NBA Player, Turned NBA Coach, **Paul Pressey**

 Former All-Pro NFL Player, **Justin Forsett**

 Best-Selling Author, Podcast Host And Entrepreneurship Educator,

Grant Cardone

» In what areas of your life could you be more consistent? _____

» In what areas of your life are you the most consistent? _____

....

"Seest thou a man diligent in his business? he shall stand before kings; he shall not stand before mean men."

PROVERBS 22:29

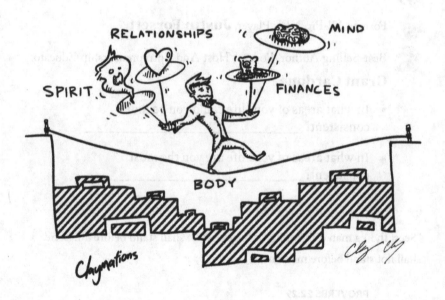

CHAPTER 10:

WHAT GETS SCHEDULED GETS DONE

In order to become a successful entrepreneur you must master the following SUPER MOVES listed below. They are not complicated, but they do require self-discipline and organization.

Super Move #1

Stop Hanging Around Idiots

You must accept that you will become the average of the five people that you spend the most time with.

....

"He that walketh with wise men shall be wise: but a companion of fools shall be destroyed."

Proverbs 10:4

Super Move #2

Carry A To-Do List At All Times

When you don't carry a to-do list it becomes very easy to waste your time doing things that don't matter. You will become known as the person who is forgetful, unreliable, and untrustworthy. If your desire is to be promoted you must up your game when it comes to becoming an organized and proactive person. Every day before you see another human, it is essential that you create a to-do list with your daily action items on it.

....

FUN FACT:

"U.S. adults now spend nearly half a day interacting with media. American adults spend over 11 hours per day listening to, watching, reading or generally interacting with media."

https://www.nielsen.com/insights/2018/time-flies-us-adults-now-spend-nearly-half-a-day-interacting-with-media/

Super Move #3

Carry A Printed Version Of
Today's Calendar At All Times

As you move up, you will have more and more responsibilities put on your plate. In order not to forget something important, it is imperative for your success that you carry a printed copy of your calendar at all times. As an example, I sincerely have no idea what I am supposed to do tomorrow, but my calendar knows, so I print it off daily.

....

"What gets scheduled gets done."

LEE COCKERELL

(The former Executive Vice President of Walt Disney World Resorts who once managed over 40,000 cast members/employees)

Super Move #4

Don't Have Sex With Someone You Just Met or People Who Are Not Your Wife

Over the years, I have personally watched family, friends, and other people throw their entire careers away for a regrettable and passionate night with someone they just met. Soon, they find out that they have a disease or a child on the way and they begin to find their lives filled with chaos. When in doubt, don't have sex with someone you just met. Know where you are going and go there and avoid lascivious people who are drifting sexually.

....

"The world has the habit of making room for the man whose actions show that he knows where he is going."

- NAPOLEON HILL

(The best-selling author of Think & Grow Rich. The book Think & Grow Rich changed my life and I named my son after him, Aubrey Napoleon-Hill Clark.)

Super Move #5

Always Know Your Goals

When you go out of your way to always be in tune and aware of your goals, setting yourself apart from most people who simply work for a check. When you know the company's goals you will find yourself coming up with new ideas to make the company more efficient and more profitable.

....

"There is one quality which one must possess to win, and that is definiteness of purpose, the knowledge of what one wants, and a burning desire to possess it."

- NAPOLEON HILL

(A man who was mentored directly by the steel tycoon Andrew Carnegie, the best-selling self-help author of all-time during his lifetime, the author of Think & Grow Rich, The Law of Success, The Master-Key to Riches, etc...)

Super Move #6

Do What You Have To Do To Wow Your Customers

Bottom Line, customers are the boss and you must assume that the ball is always being dropped. You must WOW your customers. If you want to get promoted and achieve super levels of success, you must obsess about wowing your customers, clients and patrons.

"Only the paranoid survive."

ANDY GROVE

(Under Andy Grove's leadership, Intel became the world's largest chip maker and one of the most admired companies in the world. In Only the Paranoid Survive, Grove reveals his strategy for measuring the nightmare moment every leader dreads--when massive change occurs and a company must, virtually overnight, adapt or fall by the wayside--in a new way.)

Super Move #7

View Work as "Worship" and Not Just As A Job

The Old Testament of the Bible was written in Hebrew. In Hebrew, the word "work" and the word "worship" mean the same thing. Thus, when God told Adam to "work in the garden", he was telling Adam that his work ethic was the best way for Adam to give praise and "worship" to his creator. In order to achieve his massive success, you must learn how to view your "work" as your "worship."

To learn more about this concept listen to my interviews with Rabbi Daniel Lapin:

https://www.ThrivetimeShow.com/Podcast-Guests/Rabbi-Daniel-Lapin/

Super Move #8

If you want to get promoted in the marketplace you need to get noticed (for doing the right things). You simply cannot just show up to work on time and do your job and expect to get that job promotion you've been looking for. In order to get that promotion, you have to get your boss's attention. When you exceed your clients expectations you will WOW them.

....

"If you're remarkable, it's likely that some people won't like you. That's part of the definition of remarkable. Nobody gets unanimous praise–ever. The best the timid can hope for is to be unnoticed. Criticism comes to those who stand out."

SETH GODIN

(Born in 1977, Godin worked at a bagel factory that produced everything bagels. After leaving Spinnaker in 1986, he used $20,000 in savings to establish Seth Godin Productions, which primarily operated as a book packaging business. He operated this venture out of a studio apartment in New York City. He then met Mark Hurst and founded Yoyodyne (named in jest after the fictional Yoyodyne in The Adventures of Buckaroo Banzai Across the 8th Dimension. In 1998, he sold Yoyodyne to Yahoo! for about $30 million.)

Super Move #9

Complete All Projects Early And Use Checklists for Everything

When you commit to turning in all work projects early you get known as a person that can be counted on and that is powerful. When you turn in projects on time or barely on time, you are not standing out and you are not going in the right direction if your goal is winning in the marketplace. If you miss deadlines your career is dead and you will not get ahead.

"The volume and complexity of what we know has exceeded our individual ability to deliver its benefits correctly, safely, or reliably. We don't like checklists. They can be painstaking. They're not much fun. But I don't think the issue here is mere laziness. There's something deeper, more visceral going on when people walk away not only from saving lives but from making money. It somehow feels beneath us to use a checklist, an embarrassment. It runs counter to deeply held beliefs about how the truly great among us—those we aspire to be—handle situations of high stakes and complexity. The truly great are daring. They improvise. They do not have protocols and checklists. Maybe our idea of heroism needs updating."

ATUL GAWANDE

(The best-selling author of The Checklist Manifesto: How to Get Things Right, a renowned surgeon, writer, and public health leader. Prior to joining the Biden-Harris administration, he was a practicing general and endocrine surgeon at Brigham and Women's Hospital and a professor at Harvard Medical School and the Harvard T.H. Chan School of Public Health.)

Super Move #10

Bring Great Energy To Work

Nobody wants to work with a "mopey" person and a "whiny" person. Customers don't want to buy from low energy people. Employees don't want to be managed by negative and angry bosses. Volunteers cannot be inspired by passionless leaders. If you want to succeed, you must dig deep down and find that great energy every day before you come into the workplace.

"You can start right where you stand and apply the habit of going the extra mile by rendering more service and better service than you are now being paid for."

NAPOLEON HILL

(A man who was mentored directly by the steel tycoon Andrew Carnegie, the best-selling self-help author of all-time during his lifetime, the author of Think & Grow Rich, The Law of Success, The Master-Key to Riches, etc...)

Super Move #11

Determine To Be In The Top 5% Of Your Industry

Regardless of what the people around you are up to, YOU must focus on becoming the best "YOU" can be. Don't worry or even think about the people around you that might be "mailing it in", and "doing just enough not to get fired". You personally must focus on being in the top 5% of your industry. How can you get better? How can you improve your performance?

"About half of the salespeople I've worked with over the years gave up after a single rejection. They would call a client, the client would say no, and the salesperson would never call that person back. Very few, perhaps only 4 percent to 5 percent, keep trying after four rejections. Yet, as you learned in the previous chapter, I've found that it takes about 8.4 rejections to get a meeting. And what makes the difference between people who will face that rejection one time and quit or 40 times and never quit is determined purely by the strength of their ego."

CHET HOLMES

(The iconic sales trainer, business growth consultant and the best-selling author of The Ultimate Sales Machine: Turbocharge Your Business with Relentless Focus on 12 Key Strategies)

Super Move #12

Wear A Smile All Day

When you look pissed, you repel promotions, opportunities, and promotion. No matter what you are going through, make it your mission to keep your face in the happy optimistic position. A smile says to the world, "I am looking for promotion, success, and to be my best." A frown or the absence of a smile says "Stay away from me. What I have might be contagious."

....

"There is one quality which one must possess to win, and that is definiteness of purpose, the knowledge of what one wants, and a burning desire to possess it."

NAPOLEON HILL
(Best-selling author of Think and Grow Rich and the former speech writer to President Franklin Delano Roosevelt)

Super Move #13

Become A Notetaker

If your quest is to be the best you must begin taking notes. Good bosses are busy and top-level managers are always fast-moving, thus they do not like to have to repeat themselves. When your boss speaks, take notes and write down what they are saying so that you don't have to ask them the same thing repeatedly.

"Genius is 1 percent inspiration, and 99 percent perspiration."

THOMAS EDISON

(The legendary inventor whose team created the first practical light bulb, the first recorded audio, and the motion picture technology while creating General Electric)

Super Move #14

Leave Your Personal Problems At Home

We all have personal problems. In the past 10 years, my wife and I have dealt with a miscarriage, the death of close family, cancer in the family, and losing my dad to the ravages of Lou Gehrig's disease, family members misusing company funds, employees sleeping with employees, and theft. We don't use these events and unfortunate situations to justify missing work, payroll, etc. No matter what is happening in your personal life, do your job.

"To know thyself is the beginning of wisdom."

SOCRATES

(A classical Greek philosopher who was credited as being one of the founders of modern Western Philosophy)

Super Move #15

Only Focus On Wowing Your Boss and the Clients

If you want to dominate at work, you must focus on only wowing your boss and your customers. Some people are going to try and distract you, annoy you, and even sabotage you. However, if you will focus on just wowing your boss and your customers you will win.

....

"Face reality as it is, not as it was or as you wish it to be."

JACK WELCH

(The CEO who grew GE by 4,000% during his tenure)

"27 Idle hands are the devil's workshop; idle lips are his mouthpiece. 28 An evil man sows strife; gossip separates the best of friends. 29 Wickedness loves company—and leads others into sin."

PROVERBS 16:27-29

Super Move #16

Energize and Encourage The People Around You

It only takes a few quick seconds, but bosses notice the employees who compliment and encourages those around them. Take a moment each day and write down something positive and sincere to say about the team members around you. When the time is appropriate, compliment the people around you and cheer for their success.

"Every adversity brings with it the seed of an equivalent advantage."

NAPOLEON HILL

(A man who was mentored directly by the steel tycoon Andrew Carnegie, the best-selling self-help author of all-time during his lifetime, the author of Think & Grow Rich, The Law of Success, The Master-Key to Riches, etc...)

Super Move #17

Become Known As An Organized Person

When you are an organized person you cause your boss and customers to trust you. When you are always scrounging around looking for that "thing", and trying to find that "piece of paper" that has all the passwords on it, you will quickly become written off as an unpromotable person. Stay organized and you will find yourself on the path to promotion.

"In fact, what determines your wealth is not how much you make but how much you keep of what you make."

DAVID BACH

(New York Times best-selling author of Automatic Millionaire)

Super Move #18

Ask Successful People What Books To Read (And Read Them)

You will become the average of the 5 people you spend the most time with and your mindset will be greatly impacted by the books you read. Ask successful people what business books have impacted their career and life the most and then read those books. Apply the principles found within those books and you will win.

....

"Education is the key to unlock the golden door of freedom."

 GEORGE WASHINGTON CARVER

(The famous botanist who was born a slave and went on to completely revolutionize the way Americans farm)

Super Move #19

Get Enough Sleep

When you come to work looking like death, that is not a "good look."

Everyone around you will come up to you and ask "Karl, what's wrong?" and "Janet, what's going on? Are you ok?"

People cannot stand employees who always come to work looking "rough". To succeed you need energy. Turn off Netflix, Amazon video streaming, your video games, and go to bed by 10 PM.

"Self-discipline begins with the mastery of your thoughts. If you don't control what you think, you can't control what you do. Simply, self-discipline enables you to think first and act afterward."

NAPOLEON HILL

(The legendary author of Think & Grow Rich and the best-selling self-help author of his lifetime. Napoleon Hill's book Think & Grow Rich changed my life so I named my son Aubrey Napoleon-Hill Clark and I don't regret it at all.)

Super Move #20

Be Funny (Or At Least Attempt To Be)

Every workplace is going to have its ups and downs. But it is possible to find the positive elements or the humor in nearly any situation. Choose to be the person with the Chuck Norris jokes to lighten the mood of the self-deprecating humor to make those around you laugh at your expense. Remember, a spoonful of sugar makes the medicine go down.

"*TIME IS THE SCARCEST RESOURCE OF THE MANAGER;
IF IT IS NOT MANAGED, NOTHING ELSE CAN BE MANAGED.*"
- PETER F. DRUCKER

CHAPTER 11:

CASH IS KING

If you do not choose to develop the habit of saving money you will always find yourself in a tough spot financially.

....

"If you cannot save, then the seeds of greatness are not within you."

W. CLEMENT STONE

(Stone was born in Chicago, Illinois, on May 4, 1902. His father died in 1905 leaving his family in debt. In 1908 he hawked newspapers on the South Side of Chicago while his mother worked as a dressmaker. By 1915 he owned his own newsstand. In 1918 he moved to Detroit to sell casualty insurance for his mother. In 1919, he graduated to selling insurance policies in downtown business offices. His mother managed his new career. Then in 1922, he opened his own small insurance agency, Combined Registry Company, in Chicago. By 1930, he had over 1000 agents selling insurance for him across the United States. In 1947, after his business had grown significantly, Stone built the Combined Insurance Company of America, which provided both accident and health insurance coverage. By 1979, his insurance company exceeded $1 billion in assets. Combined later merged with the Ryan Insurance Group to form Aon Corporation in 1987, and Combined was later spun off by Aon to ACE Limited in April 2008 for $2.56 billion.)

The first time I read the above quote by W. Clement Stone I remember getting angry. I then vividly remember begging my wife's boss at the time, Doctor Robert Zoellner, to meet me so that I could pick his brain on the best ways to get the capital needed to grow my company, DJConnection.com. As a result of lowering his standards, Doctor Zoellner agreed to meet with me at Ruby Tuesdays. I remember looking at Doctor Zoellner and asking him where he got the money to start www.DrZoellner.com and what advice he would have for me on where I should get the capital needed to start my business.

Doctor Zoellner told me that he worked multiple jobs and even worked as a dishwasher at a Mexican restaurant in route to saving up the money he needed to start his successful optometry clinic. He explained to me that he worked 7 days per week in order to save up the money to start his own optometry clinic. He then explained that once he opened his own business he also worked 7 days per week to make the business profitable. Thus, I decided that was what I was going to have to do as well.

Soon after I applied for a job at any place that I could think of and quickly landed jobs at Applebee's, Target, and DirecTV.

My friend, you and I must determine right now that we will develop the habit of saving money so that we can become super successful. I sincerely believe that money is just a magnifier and it makes you and I more of who we are and who we want to be. If you are generous, money simply allows you to be generous at scale. If you are a kind person, money simply allows you to be kind at scale. Most of us can't perpetually move back in with our figurative brother-in-law every time we ruin our relationships and our finances.

We must be responsible with our finances.

....

"Your words become your actions. Your actions become your habits. Your habits become your values. Your values become your destiny."

MAHATMA GANDHI

(An Indian lawyer, anti-colonial nationalist, and political ethicist who employed nonviolent resistance to lead the successful campaign for India's independence from British rule. He inspired movements for civil rights and freedom across the world.)

"You can start right where you stand and apply the habit of going the extra mile by rendering more service and better service than you are now being paid for."

NAPOLEON HILL

(A man who was mentored directly by the steel tycoon Andrew Carnegie, the best-selling self-help author of all-time during his lifetime, the author of Think & Grow Rich, The Law of Success, The Master-Key to Riches, etc...)

When starting Elephant In The Room Men's Grooming Lounge and every other company I have coached or started, I focus on how we can systematically WOW great customers like YOU. As I design the workflows, I am constantly thinking about what we can do to take the customer experience to the next level. However, when I start a company, I usually do not know the entire industry both inside and out. When I started DJConnection.com and grew it into one of America's largest wedding and corporate entertainment companies I did not know the ins and outs of the business, but I did know the pattern of entrepreneurship, which is:

Becoming successful is a result of:

1. **Finding a problem that your ideal and likely buyers have**

2. **Creating a solution that your ideal and likely buyers love**

3. **Selling the solution for your ideal and likely buyers**

4. **Nailing and scaling the solution that you are selling to your ideal and likely buyers**

5. **You too can have massive success, but you must determine that today is the day you are going to start.**

 "MAKE A PLACE FOR EVERYTHING."
-CLAY CLARK

"To build a successful organization you must be organized."

NAPOLEON HILL

(A man who was mentored directly by the steel tycoon Andrew Carnegie, the best-selling self-help author of all-time during his lifetime, the author of Think & Grow Rich, The Law of Success, The Master-Key to Riches, etc...)

CHAPTER 12:

START WHERE YOU STAND WITH THE TOOLS YOU HAVE

"You can start right where you stand and apply the habit of going the extra mile by rendering more service and better service than you are now being paid for."

NAPOLEON HILL

(Best-selling author of Think and Grow Rich and the former speech writer to President Franklin Delano Roosevelt)

You, too, have tenacity and the capacity to become super-successful. Having worked with thousands of clients to help them achieve massive success, I know that, you too, have the ability to start and grow a successful business.

However, do YOU believe it?

Becoming successful is a result of:

» Finding a problem that your ideal
and likely buyers have

» Creating a solution that your
ideal and likely buyers love

» Selling the solution for your
ideal and likely buyers

» Nailing and scaling the solution that you
are selling to your ideal and likely buyers

This can be your year to thrive, but will you decide to become passionate about blocking out the time on a daily basis to improve in the following areas of your life?

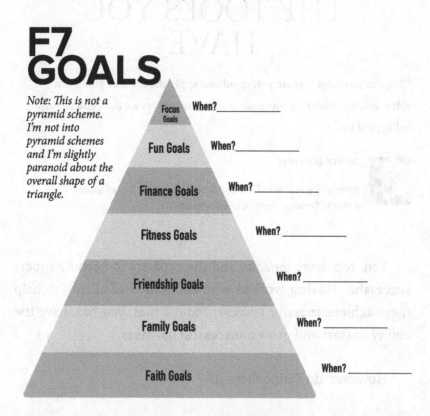

F7
GOALS

Note: This is not a pyramid scheme. I'm not into pyramid schemes and I'm slightly paranoid about the overall shape of a triangle.

Focus Goals — When?_____

Fun Goals — When?_____

Finance Goals — When?_____

Fitness Goals — When?_____

Friendship Goals — When?_____

Family Goals — When?_____

Faith Goals — When?_____

"I HELP REAL BUSINESS OWNERS TO CREATE REAL SUCCESS BY IMPLEMENTING REAL SYSTEMS THAT REALLY WORK. Motivation Is the Emotion You Receive As a Reward of Implementing the Proven Processes, Success Strategies and Best-Practice Systems That Produce Results."

"DILIGENCE, COACHABILITY, AND ATTENTION TO DETAIL ARE THE DIFFERENCE MAKERS."
- CLAY CLARK

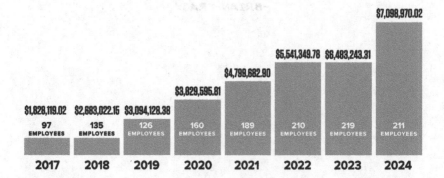

MULTI ◆ CLEAN

Year	Revenue	Employees
2017	$1,828,119.02	97 EMPLOYEES
2018	$2,683,022.15	135 EMPLOYEES
2019	$3,094,128.38	126 EMPLOYEES
2020	$3,829,595.81	160 EMPLOYEES
2021	$4,799,682.90	189 EMPLOYEES
2022	$5,541,349.78	210 EMPLOYEES
2023	$6,483,243.31	219 EMPLOYEES
2024	$7,098,970.02	211 EMPLOYEES

KEVIN THOMAS
OWNER
www.MultiCleanOk.com

CHAPTER 14:

INTENTIONALLY DESIGN THE LIFE YOU WANT TO LIVE

Today I have 5 kids and 1 wonderful wife. This was intentional. It is very, very, very important that you invest the time to think about your life and what it would be if it was perfect. Then you and I must diligently work towards achieving that goal little by little day after day. You will become the average of the 5 people you spend the most time with and your mindset will be greatly impacted by the books you read. Ask super successful people what books have impacted their career and life the most and then read those books. Apply the principles found within those books and you will win.

YOUR BUSINESS EXISTS TO SOLVE PROBLEMS
FOR YOU AND YOUR CUSTOMERS.
– CLAY CLARK

"I noticed that the dynamic range between what an average person could accomplish and what the best person could accomplish was 50 or 100 to 1. Given that, you're well advised to go after the cream of the cream … A small team of A-players can run circles around a giant team of B and C players."

STEVE JOBS

(The legendary co-founder of Apple and the man who introduced the personal computer, the iPod, the iPhone and the iPad. Steve Jobs wanted the packaging of Apple products to be so good that people would not want to throw it away without knowing why.)

CHAPTER 15:

A BUSINESS EXISTS TO SERVE YOU AS THE BUSINESS OWNER AS A RESULT OF SOLVING PROBLEMS & WOWING YOUR IDEAL & LIKELY BUYERS

In order for you and I to create both time and financial freedom we must focus on WOWING each and every customer we transact with. Now this is easier said than done, but that must be our goal. As we have grown Elephant In The Room Men's Grooming Lounge, I have always made it my goal to hire the best possible employees and to provide them with the best work environment possible so that we can WOW great people like you. Thus, every week I personally interview job applicants at 5:30 PM on Wednesday and 5:30 PM on Friday. I am on a never ending quest to hire the best!

"DON'T LET SCHOOLING INTERFERE WITH YOUR EDUCATION."
– MARK TWAIN

CHAPTER 16:

WHY EDUCATED IDIOTS WILL MAKE YOU DUMB BY DEFAULT

Not to discourage you, but to encourage you I have listed some pretty mind-numbing statistics about the status of how our lives will become by default if we are not intentional about not surrounding ourselves with idiots and drifting through life.

FUN FACTS:

According to Inc. Magazine, 85% of job applicants lie on their resumes.

https://www.inc.com/jt-odonnell/staggering-85-of-job-applicants-lying-on-resumes-.html

According to the U.S. Chamber and CBS News, 75% of employees steal from the workplace and most do so repeatedly.

https://www.cbsnews.com/news/employee-theft-are-you-blind-to-it/

According to Inc. Magazine, 96% of businesses fail within 10 years.

https://www.inc.com/bill-carmody/why-96-of-businesses-fail-within-10-years.html

You simply must choose to intentionally seek out wisdom from successful people who are achieving success in the areas where you want to achieve success. As an example:

- If you are wanting to improve the level of fitness in your life, find a personal trainer or fitness class that will push you to become your best.

- If you are looking to get a great haircut, find a men's grooming business that provides you with a better haircut than you could give yourself.

- If you are wanting your car to work properly, find a mechanic that is proven and that can get your car working properly.

- If you are looking to become a successful entrepreneur, study successful entrepreneurs.

My friend, YOU CAN DO IT!

"EVERYDAY, WAKE UP BEFORE EVERYONE
ELSE IN YOUR HOME DOES."
- CLAY CLARK

CHAPTER 17:

IF YOU ARE GOING THROUGH HELL DON'T STOP

Achieving success can often feel like you are walking through the fog and all you can see is a source of light in the distance. However, you must start somewhere. You must wake up every morning and ask yourself where you want to be. You must constantly ask yourself where you are versus where you want to be and then you must diligently press forward with big overwhelming optimistic momentum.

....

FUN FACTS:

"You cannot control what happens to you, but you can control your attitude toward what happens to you, and in that, you will be mastering change rather than allowing it to master you."

BRIAN TRACY
(The legendary best-selling author, speaker and business growth trainer)

MAKE YOUR PRIORITIES SCARED

"EAT THE BIGGEST FROG FIRST"
-BRIAN TRACY

"Discipline is the bridge between goals and accomplishments"

JIM ROHN

(Jim Rohn was an American entrepreneur, author, and motivational speaker. He wrote numerous books including How to obtain wealth and happiness. Rohn mentored Mark R. Hughes and life strategist Tony Robbins in the late 1970s. Others who credit Rohn for influencing their careers include authors/lecturers Mark Victor Hansen and Jack Canfield (Chicken Soup book series), Everton Edwards (Hallmark Innovators Conglomerate), Brian Tracy, Darren Hardy, and Harv Eker. Rohn coauthored the novel Twelve Pillars with Chris Widener.)

CHAPTER 18:

WHAT YOU NEED TO DO IS USUALLY UNRELATED TO WHAT YOU MUST DO

Every morning when I wake up and I discover that it is again 3 AM, I think to myself, "Why do I wake up this early?" However, once I start developing personal momentum before 8 AM and once I start knocking out my to-do list I begin to feel very happy with my daily decision to wake up every day at 3 AM. Oftentimes when I go to bed at 9 PM, I find myself not liking these decisions. However, when my alarm wakes me up every day at AM, I am glad that I decided to go to bed at 9 PM. So often self-discipline in our lives is the bridge between where we are and where we want to be.

"I HELP REAL BUSINESS OWNERS TO CREATE REAL SUCCESS BY IMPLEMENTING REAL SYSTEMS THAT REALLY WORK.

Motivation Is the Emotion You Receive As a Reward of Implementing the Proven Processes, Success Strategies and Best-Practice Systems That Produce Results."

"DILIGENCE, COACHABILITY, AND ATTENTION TO DETAIL ARE THE DIFFERENCE MAKERS."
- CLAY CLARK

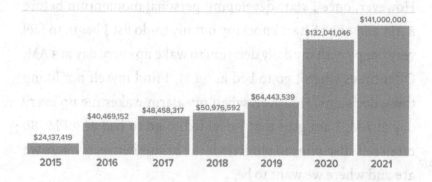

$24,137,419	$40,469,152	$48,458,317	$50,976,592	$64,443,539		$132,041,046	$141,000,000
2015	2016	2017	2018	2019	2020	2021

GLEN SHAW & AARON ANTIS
SHAW HOMES
www.ShawHomes.com

CHAPTER 19:

YOU MUST BECOME A POLYMATH TO BECOME PROFOUNDLY SUCCESSFUL IN BUSINESS

In order to become a successful entrepreneur you must become a polymath. However, what is a polymath? A polymath is a person who has experience, knowledge and often even mastery at many skills.

In order to become a successful entrepreneur you must become a master at branding, marketing, sales, workflow design, finance, accounting, management, human resources, real estate, investing, time management, search engine optimization, social media marketing and more. Although college teaches specialization, you must learn how to become successful in many areas to become a successful entrepreneur.

"In the future, the great division will be between those who have trained themselves to handle these complexities and those who are overwhelmed by them -- those who can acquire skills and discipline their minds and those who are irrevocably distracted by all the media around them and can never focus enough to learn."

ROBERT GREENE, MASTERY

(A guest on the ThrivetimeShow.com Podcast, An iconic author on strategy and power. When reading Robert Greene's books it is important to know that people that do not read the Bible and who do not adhere to God's laws often use The 48 Laws of Power against you in a nefarious way. I believe that it's important to know the moves that nefarious people will use against you so that you can protect yourself against the evil moves and the problems they will cause you. He has written seven international bestsellers, including The 48 Laws of Power, The Art of Seduction, The 33 Strategies of War, The 50th Law (with rapper 50 Cent), Mastery, The Laws of Human Nature, and The Daily Laws.)

Want to Grow a Sustainably Successful Business?

» Step 1 - Establish Your Revenue Goals

» Step 2 - Determine Your Break-Even Numbers

» Step 3 - Define the Number of Hours Per Week You Are Willing to Work

» Step 4 - Define Your Unique Value Proposition

» Step 5 - Improve Branding

» Step 6 - Create 3-Legged Marketing Stool & a Powerful No-Brainer

» Step 7 - Create a Sales Conversion System

> » Step 8 - Determine Sustainable
> Customer Acquisition Costs

> » Step 9 - Create Repeatable Systems,
> Processes & File Organization

> » Step 10 - Create Management Execution Systems

> » Step 11 - Create a Sustainable &
> Repetitive Weekly Schedule

> » Step 12 - Create Human Resources
> & Recruitment Systems

> » Step 13 - Create Accounting &
> Automate Earning Millions

> » Step 14 - Determine the Point of
> Achieving Financial Success

Remember, if you are reading this book and you feel stuck, and you are in need of coaching, connections and capital, I would highly recommend that you attend one of our in-person two-day interactive business growth workshops. As an Elephant In The Room Men's Grooming Lounge member you can claim your complimentary tickets to our next 2-Day interactive business growth workshop at www.ThrivetimeShow.com.

"I HELP REAL BUSINESS OWNERS TO CREATE REAL SUCCESS BY IMPLEMENTING REAL SYSTEMS THAT REALLY WORK.

Motivation Is the Emotion You Receive As a Reward of Implementing the Proven Processes, Success Strategies and Best-Practice Systems That Produce Results."

"DILIGENCE, COACHABILITY, AND ATTENTION TO DETAIL ARE THE DIFFERENCE MAKERS."
- CLAY CLARK

"We Have Grown 15X! We Now Have a 90% Conversion Rate. It's Made Our Business Turn-Key...Used to Take 12 Hours Per Day to Run Back-End of the Business, Now Takes 45 Minutes Per Day."

PLACID AJOKU
FOUNDER
www.BuiltPhoenixStrong.org

CHAPTER 20:

THE FOUR STEPS OF ENTREPRENEURSHIP

» Step 1 - Find Problems You Can Solve

» Step 2 - Find Solutions You Can Solve

» Step 3 - Sell the Solutions That You Provide

» Step 4 - Nail It & Scale It

When I started www.DJConnection.com my focus was on wowing brides, event planners and event attendees with great entertainment, sound and lights!

When I started www.EITRLounge.com my focus was on wowing the men who came into our Elephant In The Room Men's Grooming Lounges with the best men's grooming experience and overall atmosphere possible!

When I started www.EpicPhotos.com my focus was on wowing brides, and the people paying us by providing the best photography and videography services possible!

When I started www.MakeYourLifeEpic.com my focus was on helping entrepreneurs to dramatically grow their business!

When I co-founded www.MakeYourDogEpic.com my focus was on wowing dog owners by making sure that our team could deliver the best dog training experience on the planet!

However, once you can wow customers, now it is time to build the systems and processes needed to successfully and sustainably grow a business.

....

"If your business depends on you, you don't own a business—you have a job. And it's the worst job in the world because you're working for a lunatic!"

MICHAEL GERBER

(A ThrivetimeShow.com Podcast guest, and the legendary best-selling author of The E-Myth book series)

Building systems is not the fun part about growing a company. Building systems involves building checklists, processes, documents and diagrams that people who are not you can follow to WOW you customers repeatedly time and time again.

"ENTREPRENEURS SOLVE THE WORLD'S PROBLEMS
AND UNAPOLOGETICALLY MAKE MONEY DOING IT."
- CLAY CLARK

"EVERYTHING ELSE BECOMES UNNECESSARY IN A
BUSINESS IF NOBODY SELLS ANYTHING."
- CLAY CLARK

CHAPTER 21:

IF YOU CANNOT SELL YOUR BUSINESS WILL GO TO HELL

Years ago I met a young man that was focused on opening a sports training facility, then a power washing company, then a marketing company and then an (insert the blank company). This young man was what I call a "Happy Hoper" and new idea guy. He would hop from woman to woman, from new idea to new idea while never gaining true traction with any relationship or business. Why? Because he was addicted to new things. In order to gain traction with your business you must obsessively focus on your business for at least three years. You must wake up thinking about your business and how you can WOW your ideal and likely buyers.

"I HELP REAL BUSINESS OWNERS TO CREATE REAL SUCCESS BY IMPLEMENTING REAL SYSTEMS THAT REALLY WORK.
Motivation Is the Emotion You Receive As a Reward of Implementing the Proven Processes, Success Strategies and Best-Practice Systems That Produce Results."

"DILIGENCE, COACHABILITY, AND ATTENTION TO DETAIL ARE THE DIFFERENCE MAKERS."
- CLAY CLARK

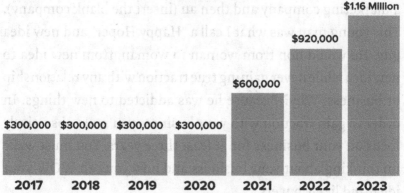

LEEAH CALVERT
FOUNDER
www.918DesignCompany.com

"Most people are sitting on their own diamond mines. The surest ways to lose your diamond mine are to get bored, become overambitious, or start thinking that the grass is greener on the other side. Find your core focus, stick to it, and devote your time and resources to excelling at it."

GINO WICKMAN

(Gino Wickman has been a multiple time guest on the ThrivetimeShow.com podcast and is known as one of the world's leading high level business consultants. He is the best-selling author of numerous books including Traction: Get a Grip On Your Business.)

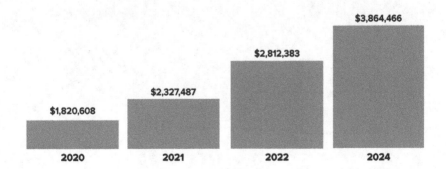

ROY COGGESHALL
FOUNDER
www.RCAutoSpecialists.com

"EXPECT MORE THAN OTHERS THINK POSSIBLE."
- HOWARD SCHULTZ (FOUNDER OF STARBUCKS)

CHAPTER 22:

HOLD YOURSELF & OTHERS TO HIGH STANDARDS OR YOU WILL DRIFT INTO MEDIOCRITY

As we have grown Elephant In The Room Men's Grooming Lounge over these past 14 years I am constantly obsessed with hiring the best stylists and grooming professionals that we can find. I am constantly looking for more and better ways to wow our customers and I am constantly asking how we can raise the bar to provide the best experience possible to great people like you and this requires daily diligence, consistency and focus.

....

"Be a yardstick of quality. Some people aren't used to an environment where excellence is expected."

STEVE JOBS

(The legendary co-founder of Apple and the man who introduced the personal computer, the iPod, the iPhone and the iPad. Steve Jobs wanted the packaging of Apple products to be so good that people would not want to throw it away without knowing why.)

"FACE REALITY AS IT IS, NOT AS IT WAS
OR AS YOU WISH IT TO BE."
- JACK WELCH

CHAPTER 23:

DISCOVER WHAT THE REAL PROBLEM IS THEN FIX IT

As I have grown Elephant In The Room Men's Grooming Lounge and countless brands over the years, I have often found that the real problem is different from the problem being described. As an example, I was told a few years back that one of our locations did not have enough parking. However, once I went to see the situation with my own eyes I found that a large homeless encampment had taken over our parking lot. I was told a few weeks ago that our drier was not working and upon further review I discovered that the lent trap had simply not been cleaned out in several weeks. As business people you and I must gather those facts then act.

"I HELP REAL BUSINESS OWNERS TO CREATE REAL SUCCESS BY IMPLEMENTING REAL SYSTEMS THAT REALLY WORK. Motivation Is the Emotion You Receive As a Reward of Implementing the Proven Processes, Success Strategies and Best-Practice Systems That Produce Results."

"DILIGENCE, COACHABILITY, AND ATTENTION TO DETAIL ARE THE DIFFERENCE MAKERS."
- CLAY CLARK

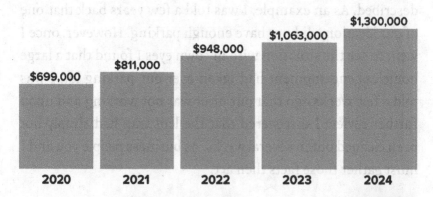

$699,000 — 2020
$811,000 — 2021
$948,000 — 2022
$1,063,000 — 2023
$1,300,000 — 2024

KENNY & DANIELLE SUTHERLAND
FOUNDER
www.HighwayManSigns.com

"It's the little things that make the big things possible. Only close attention to the fine details of any operation makes the operation first class."

JOHN WILLARD MARRIOTT SR.

(An American entrepreneur and businessman. He was the founder of the Marriott Corporation (which became Marriott International in 1993), the parent company of the world's largest hospitality, hotel chains, and food services companies. The Marriott company rose from a small root beer stand in Washington, D.C., in 1927 to a chain of family restaurants by 1932, to its first motel in 1957. By the time he died in 1985, the Marriott company operated 1,400 restaurants and 143 hotels and resorts worldwide, including two theme parks, earning US$4.5 billion in revenue annually with 154,600 employees.)

PLOT YOUR COURSE OR YOU WILL NEVER GET THERE

CHAPTER 24:

TO BUILD A SUCCESSFUL ORGANIZATION YOU MUST BE ORGANIZED

Being perpetually late, being unorganized and refusing to use both a to-do list and a calendar will put a cap on the level of success that you can achieve.

....

"If you realize that you're the problem, then you can change yourself, learn something and grow wiser. Don't blame other people for your problems."

ROBERT KIYOSAKI

(A multiple-time ThrivetimeShow.com podcast guest, an author who has co-written two books with America's 45th & 47th President Donald J. Trump, the legendary best-selling author of the Rich Dad Poor Dad book series, an investor, a podcaster and a man who has actually spoken live and in-person at our Thrivetime Show business growth conference in Tulsa, Oklahoma).

'MOST ENTREPRENEURS ARE MERELY TECHNICIANS WITH AN
ENTREPRENEURIAL SEIZURE. MOST ENTREPRENEURS FAIL BECAUSE THEY ARE
WORKING IN THEIR BUSINESS RATHER THAN ON THEIR BUSINESS.'
- MICHAEL GERBER

CHAPTER 25:

TO BUILD A SUCCESSFUL BUSINESS YOU CANNOT BE A MORAL REPROBATE

You can't screw partners, screw over customers, and literally screw women you are not married to, and screw up multiple marriages without screwing up your life. You must become self disciplined.

....

"You must take personal responsibility. You cannot change the circumstances, the seasons, or the wind, but you can change yourself. That is something you are in charge of."

JIM ROHN

(Jim Rohn was an American entrepreneur, author, and motivational speaker. He wrote numerous books including How to obtain wealth and happiness. Rohn mentored Mark R. Hughes and life strategist Tony Robbins in the late 1970s. Others who credit Rohn for influencing their careers include authors/lecturers Mark Victor Hansen and Jack Canfield (Chicken Soup book series), Everton Edwards (Hallmark Innovators Conglomerate), Brian Tracy, Darren Hardy, and Harv Eker. Rohn coauthored the novel Twelve Pillars with Chris Widener.)

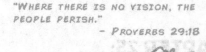

CHAPTER 26:

FOLLOW GOD'S LAWS OR YOUR LIFE WILL BECOME SIN-INSPIRED & TERRIBLE QUICKLY

None of us are perfect, and we all make mistakes. I know that every day you and I must sincerely work to improve. However, if we intentionally choose to engage in sin. Our lives are going to become terrible quickly as a direct consequence of our actions.

....

"Where there is no vision, the people perish: but he that keepeth the law, happy is he."

PROVERBS 29:18

FUN FACT:

The Ten Commandments Found In Exodus Chapter 20 Are Listed Below:

First Commandment -
"Thou shalt have no other gods before me."

Second Commandment -
"Thou shalt not make unto thee any graven image, or any likeness of any thing that is in heaven above, or that is in the earth beneath, or that is in the water under the earth: Thou shalt not bow down thyself to them, nor serve them: for I the LORD thy God am a jealous God, visiting the iniquity of the fathers upon the children unto the third and fourth generation of them that hate me; "

Third Commandment -
"Thou shalt not take the name of the LORD thy God in vain; for the LORD will not hold him guiltless that taketh his name in vain."

Fourth Commandment -
"Remember the sabbath day, to keep it holy."

Fifth Commandment -
"Honour thy father and thy mother: that thy days may be long upon the land which the LORD thy God giveth thee."

Sixth Commandment -
"Thou shalt not kill."

Seventh Commandment
"Thou shalt not commit adultery."

Eight Commandment -
"Thou shalt not steal."

Ninth Commandment -
"Thou shalt not bear false witness against thy neighbour."

Tenth Commandment -
"Thou shalt not covet thy neighbour's house, thou shalt not covet thy neighbour's wife, nor his manservant, nor his maidservant, nor his ox, nor his ass, nor any thing that is thy neighbour's."

"I HELP REAL BUSINESS OWNERS TO CREATE REAL SUCCESS BY IMPLEMENTING REAL SYSTEMS THAT REALLY WORK.

Motivation Is the Emotion You Receive As a Reward of Implementing the Proven Processes, Success Strategies and Best-Practice Systems That Produce Results."

"DILIGENCE, COACHABILITY, ANDATTENTION TO DETAIL ARE THE DIFFERENCE MAKERS."
- CLAY CLARK

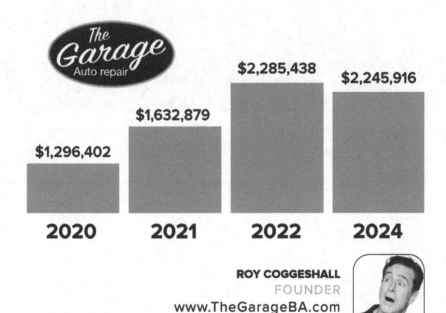

ROY COGGESHALL
FOUNDER
www.TheGarageBA.com

"TEMPORARY FAILURES ARE A PREREQUISITE TO SUCCESS."
-NAPOLEON HILL

CHAPTER 27:

FAILURE IS PREREQUISITE TO SUCCESS

"Every time I read a management or self-help book, I find myself saying, "That's fine, but that wasn't really the hard thing about the situation." The hard thing isn't setting a big, hairy, audacious goal. The hard thing is laying people off when you miss the big goal. The hard thing isn't hiring great people. The hard thing is when those "great people" develop a sense of entitlement and start demanding unreasonable things. The hard thing isn't setting up an organizational chart. The hard thing is getting people to communicate within the organization that you just designed.

The hard thing isn't dreaming big. The hard thing is waking up in the middle of the night in a cold sweat when the dream turns into a nightmare."

BEN HOROWITZ

(Ben Horowitz is an American businessman, investor, blogger, and author. He is a technology entrepreneur and co-founder of the venture capital firm Andreessen Horowitz along with Marc Andreessen. He previously co-founded and served as president and chief executive officer of the enterprise software company Opsware, which Hewlett-Packard acquired in 2007 for $1.6 billion in cash. Ben is the best-selling author of The Hard Thing About Hard Things: Building a Business When There Are No Easy Answers)

In life and in business massive setbacks are going to happen. As we were growing Elephant In The Room (as with any business), I remember watching the process during the first 3 years of virtually every early employee choosing to start a business to directly compete with Elephant In The Room Men's Grooming Lounge after we had fully trained them. I remember watching employees self-sabotage and wreck their marriages through infidelity. I remember watching key employees and teammates take jobs in different states, and I remember watching key employees wreck relationships with each other through gossip, betrayal and through financial embezzlement and misuse of company money. I actually had to watch members of my own family wreck their marriages, cheat on their spouse, and misuse company money. However, I had to decide to keep going and you must decide to keep going no matter how challenging the circumstances may look.

....

"I think it's really important to keep on staying motivated."

WOLFGANG PUCK

(ThrivetimeShow.com podcast guest, celebrity chef, entrepreneur and best-selling author).

"I HELP REAL BUSINESS OWNERS TO CREATE REAL SUCCESS BY IMPLEMENTING REAL SYSTEMS THAT REALLY WORK.
Motivation Is the Emotion You Receive As a Reward of Implementing the Proven Processes, Success Strategies and Best-Practice Systems That Produce Results."

"DILIGENCE, COACHABILITY, ANDATTENTION TO DETAIL ARE THE DIFFERENCE MAKERS."
- CLAY CLARK

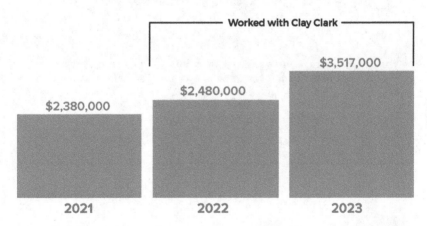

Worked with Clay Clark

	$2,480,000	$3,517,000
$2,380,000		
2021	2022	2023

PAUL HOOD
OWNER
www.HoodCPAs.com

"IN A CROWDED MARKETPLACE, FITTING IN IS FAILING. IN A
BUSY MARKETPLACE, NOT STANDING OUT IS THE SAME AS
BEING INVISIBLE."
- SETH GODIN
BEST-SELLING AUTHOR OF "PURPLE COW"

CHAPTER 28:

CHOOSE TO BE REMARKABLE, BECAUSE BY DEFAULT YOU ARE INVISIBLE

When building Elephant In The Room Men's Grooming Lounge I was very intentional about the name of the company, the branding of the company and every aspect of the marketing related to the company and you must be intentional about making sure that your business stands out amidst the clutter of commerce if you want your business to be successful as well. As entrepreneurs we must be intentional about the following aspects of our business and more:

 The sights   The smells

 The sounds   The ambiance

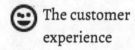 The customer experience

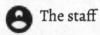 The staff

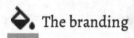 The branding

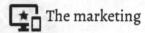 The marketing

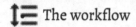 The workflow

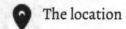 The location

"In a crowded marketplace, fitting in is failing. In a busy marketplace, not standing out is the same as being invisible. If you're remarkable, it's likely that some people won't like you. That's part of the definition of remarkable. Nobody gets unanimous praise–ever."

SETH GODIN

(Seth Godin has been a ThrivetimeShow.com podcast guest. Born in 1977, Seth Godin worked at a bagel factory that produced everything bagels. After leaving Spinnaker in 1986, he used $20,000 in savings to establish Seth Godin Productions, which primarily operated as a book packaging business. He operated this venture out of a studio apartment in New York City. He then met Mark Hurst and founded Yoyodyne (named in jest after the fictional Yoyodyne in The Adventures of Buckaroo Banzai Across the 8th Dimension. In 1998, he sold Yoyodyne to Yahoo! for about $30 million.)

CHAPTER 29:

HE THAT WALKETH WITH WISE MEN SHALL BE WISE: BUT A COMPANION OF FOOLS SHALL BE DESTROYED. PROVERBS 13:20

....

"Do not be deceived: "Evil company corrupts good habits.""

1ST CORINTHIANS 15:33

You simply cannot have success in your life if you choose to surround yourself with people who are constantly involved in drama, poor life decisions, infidelity, money-management issues and other self-inflicting poverty causing jackassery.

CHAPTER 30:

GOOD IS THE ENEMY
OF GREAT

....

"I value an entrepreneur I can get behind and trust, because I know they are attempting to move forward in life."

DAYMOND JOHN

(Daymond John has been ThrivetimeShow.com podcast guest and is a New York Times best-selling author, founder of FUBU, Shark Tank "Shark", investor, consultant and entrepreneur who turned a $40 investment into a $6 billion fashion brand FUBU.)

Early on in my career I would settle for business associates that I could not trust because I did not know how to find high character people to surround myself with. I let people that could not be trusted with being faithful to operate within my business because I thought their personal problems would not show up at the workplace, but that was wrong. In my life and in yours we must always remember that just enough is the enemy of great.

CHAPTER 31:

WHEN YOU ATTEMPT TO ESCAPE THE WAGE CAGE, YOU WILL BE ATTACKED

When you and I sign up to become self-employed we are signing up to be attacked and to be attacked relentlessly. Having been self-employed since the age of 15, I can tell you that if you are going to choose to be self-employed you are going to have to deal with the harsh reality that you will be attacked constantly.

....

"When you show yourself to the world and display your talents, you naturally stir all kinds of resentment, envy, and other manifestations of insecurity... you cannot spend your life worrying about the petty feelings of others."

ROBERT GREENE, MASTERY

(A guest on the ThrivetimeShow.com podcast, an iconic author on strategy and power. When reading Robert Greene's books it is important to know that people that do not read the Bible and who do not adhere to God's laws often use The 48 Laws of Power against you in a nefarious way. I believe that it's important to know the moves that nefarious people will use against you so that you can protect yourself against the evil moves and the problems they will cause you. He has written seven international bestsellers, including The 48 Laws of Power, The Art of Seduction, The 33 Strategies of War, The 50th Law (with rapper 50 Cent), Mastery, The Laws of Human Nature, and The Daily Laws.)

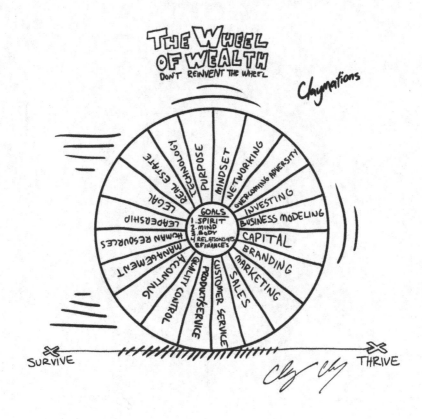

IT'S NOT ABOUT HOW MUCH YOU MAKE,
ITS ABOUT HOW MUCH YOU KEEP.
-CLAY CLARK

CHAPTER 32:

IT'S NOT HOW MUCH MONEY YOU MAKE, IT'S HOW MUCH MONEY YOU KEEP

As you run a business you must block out time each and every day to look at your numbers and to make sure that you are being profitable and that you are minimizing the amount of money being lost due to waste and fraud. You must make sure that you are tracking the results of your marketing and that you know what is working and what is not. This is a daily grind that must stay on your mind if you are to become successful as an entrepreneur on the planet Earth.

"It's not how much money you make, but how much money you keep, and how hard it works for you."

ROBERT KIYOSAKI

(A multiple-time ThrivetimeShow.com podcast guest, an author who has co-written two books with America's 45th & 47th President Donald J. Trump, the legendary best-selling author of the Rich Dad Poor Dad book series, an investor, a podcaster and a man who has actually spoken live and in-person at our Thrivetime Show business growth conference in Tulsa, Oklahoma).

CHAPTER 33:

CREATE A BUSINESS THAT IS REPEATABLE & SCALABLE OR YOU WILL FIND YOURSELF BECOMING A 24/7 EMPLOYEE WORKING NON-STOP FOR YOURSELF

As we were building The Elephant In The Room Men's Grooming Lounge I wanted to nail down every system, every checklist and every process before we opened up the second location. I wanted to nail it before we scaled it and that is what we did. Although this part of the business might not be fun it is necessary.

....

"If your business depends on you, you don't own a business—you have a job. And it's the worst job in the world because you're working for a lunatic!"

MICHAEL GERBER

(Michael Gerber is a ThrivetimeShow.com Podcast guest, and the legendary best-selling author of The E-Myth book series)

"I HELP REAL BUSINESS OWNERS TO CREATE REAL SUCCESS BY IMPLEMENTING REAL SYSTEMS THAT REALLY WORK.

Motivation Is the Emotion You Receive As a Reward of Implementing the Proven Processes, Success Strategies and Best-Practice Systems That Produce Results."

"DILIGENCE, COACHABILITY, AND ATTENTION TO DETAIL ARE THE DIFFERENCE MAKERS."
- CLAY CLARK

"Clarify your vision and you will make better decisions about people, processes, finances, strategies, and customers."

GINO WICKMAN

(Gino Wickman has been a multiple time guest on the ThrivetimeShow.com podcast and is known as one of the world's leading high level business consultants. He is the best-selling author of numerous books including Traction: Get a Grip On Your Business.)

CHAPTER 34:

CHOOSE TO LIVE BEFORE YOU DIE

It is so important that you and I invest the time needed on a daily basis to ask ourselves if we are going the right direction in our F7 life. Take a moment now and ask yourself if you are happy with the direction that you are currently going in the following areas:

Faith: _____

Family: _____

Finances: _____

Fitness: _____

Friendship: _____

Fun: _____

Focused Attention: _____

"TIME IS THE SCARCEST RESOURCE OF THE MANAGER;
IF IT IS NOT MANAGED, NOTHING ELSE CAN BE MANAGED."
- PETER F. DRUCKER

CHAPTER 35:

TIME IS YOUR MOST VALUABLE ASSET

This just in...you and I are not going to live forever on this planet Earth. Thus, let's choose to live before we die.

> » If you have a person in your life that is perpetually causing your strife, solve the problem or get them out of your life.

> » If you have a burning desire to become the world's best employee, get started wowing your boss today!

> » If you want to get in the best shape of your life, block out time to get to the gym everyday starting now!

"Remembering that I'll be dead soon is the most important tool I've ever encountered to help me make the big choices in life. Almost everything--all external expectations, all pride, all fear of embarrassment or failure--these things just fall away in the face of death, leaving only what is truly important. Remembering that you are going to die is the best way I know to avoid the trap of thinking you have something to lose. You are already naked. There is no reason not to follow your heart. No one wants to die. Even people who want to go to heaven don't want to die to get there. And yet, death is the destination we all share. No one has ever escaped it, and that is how it should be, because death is very likely the single best invention of life. It's life's change agent. It clears out the old to make way for the new."

STEVE JOBS

(The legendary co-founder of Apple and the man who introduced the personal computer, the iPod, the iPhone and the iPad. Steve Jobs wanted the packaging of Apple products to be so good that people would not want to throw it away without knowing why.)

IT'S NOT ABOUT HOW MUCH YOU MAKE.
ITS ABOUT HOW MUCH YOU KEEP.
-CLAY CLARK

"IF YOU'RE GOING TO BE THINKING ANYTHING,
YOU MIGHT AS WELL THINK BIG."
- DONALD TRUMP

CHAPTER 36:

YOU CAN'T STEER A PARKED BUS

I often quote myself on this point. My friend, the time will never be just right. You must act now.

....

"Procrastination is the giant. Action is the sword. Inspiration is the reward."

CLAY CLARK

Stop thinking that you are:

» Too young to get started.

» Too poor to get started.

» Too inexperienced to make a difference.

» Too lazy to become ambitious.

» Too overwhelmed to get organized.

» Too messed up to turn your life around.

» God did not make you by accident. Every day that we have on this Earth is a gift from God and what you and I do with it is a gift to God. This is your year to Thrive!

CHAPTER 37:

THE PATH TO PROSPERITY INVOLVES FINDING THE PROVEN PATH TO SUCCESS & THE IMPLEMENTATION OF BEST-PRACTICE BUSINESS SYSTEMS

....

"If you are the kind of person who is waiting for the 'right' thing to happen, you might wait for a long time. It's like waiting for all the traffic lights to be green for five miles before starting the trip."

ROBERT KIYOSAKI

(The best-selling author of The Rich Dad Poor Dad book series and a man who has sold over 40 million copies of his entrepreneur books. Robert is a multiple-time ThrivetimeShow.com podcast guest, an author who has co-written two books with America's 45th & 47th President Donald J. Trump, the legendary best-selling author of the Rich Dad Poor Dad book series, an investor, a podcaster and a man who has actually spoken live and in-person at our Thrivetime Show business growth conference in Tulsa, Oklahoma).

Over time I have become convinced that your network is your net worth and that you will become the average of the five people that you spend the most time with. Thus, I would recommend that you become very intentional about whom you invest your time with. I would recommend that you would begin devouring self-help books written by successful people, listening to podcasts like the ThrivetimeShow.com podcast that teach how to become successful and attending workshops like the 2-day interactive ThrivetimeShow.com business conference hosted right here in Tulsa, Oklahoma. Remember, as an Elephant In The Room Men's Grooming Lounge member you can claim your complimentary tickets to our next 2-Day interactive business growth workshop at www.ThrivetimeShow.com.

Clay Clark catching up with longtime business partner & friend, David Robinson.

The path to success can be scary, but you can do i!

CHAPTER 38:

THE MESSAGE MATTERS AS MUCH AS THE PLATFORM

If you have a burning desire to start a successful podcast or to become an influencer you must make sure that what you are teaching, showing and putting out connects with your ideal and likely buyers and your desired audience. You must become so good at your craft that people simply cannot keep themselves from telling people about you and your platform.

....

"Be so good they can't ignore you."

STEVE MARTIN

(Steve Martin is an American comedian, actor, writer, producer, and musician. Known for his work in comedy films, television, and recording, he has received many accolades, including five Grammy Awards, a Primetime Emmy Award, a Screen Actors Guild Award, and an Honorary Academy Award, in addition to nominations for two Tony Awards. He also received the Mark Twain Prize for American Humor in 2005, the Kennedy Center Honors in 2007, and an AFI Life Achievement Award in 2015. In 2004, Comedy Central ranked Martin at sixth place in a list of the 100 greatest stand-up comics. He then starred in films such as The Jerk (1979), Dead Men Don't Wear Plaid (1982), The Man with Two Brains (1983), All of Me (1984), ¡Three Amigos! (1986), Planes, Trains and Automobiles (1987), Dirty Rotten Scoundrels (1988), L.A. Story (1991), Bowfinger (1999) and Looney Tunes: Back in Action (2003). He played family patriarchs in Parenthood (1989), the Father of the Bride films (1991-1995), Bringing Down the House (2003), and the Cheaper by the Dozen films (2003-2005).

"I HELP REAL BUSINESS OWNERS TO CREATE REAL SUCCESS BY IMPLEMENTING REAL SYSTEMS THAT REALLY WORK.
Motivation Is the Emotion You Receive As a Reward of Implementing the Proven Processes, Success Strategies and Best-Practice Systems That Produce Results."

"DILIGENCE, COACHABILITY, AND ATTENTION TO DETAIL ARE THE DIFFERENCE MAKERS."
- CLAY CLARK

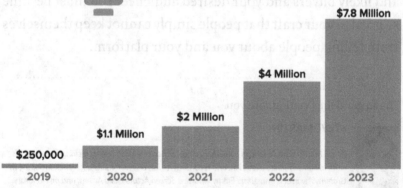

$7.8 Million — 2023
$4 Million — 2022
$2 Million — 2021
$1.1 Milion — 2020
$250,000 — 2019

JEFF HANSON
OWNER / FOUNDER
www.Concord-Home.com.com

CHAPTER 39:

FOCUS ON ONLY WHAT YOU CAN CONTROL

Over the past 14 years we have ran The Elephant In The Room I have focused on the fact that I cannot control the weather, I cannot control the emotions of other people, I cannot control the economy, but I can focus on trying to WOW great customers like you by providing a great atmosphere, a great team and great quality haircuts.

....

"Life is much easier for everyone when you have people around you who genuinely get it, want it, and have the capacity to do it."

GINO WICKMAN

(Gino Wickman has been a multiple time guest on the ThrivetimeShow.com podcast and is known as one of the world's leading high level business consultants. He is the best-selling author of numerous books including Traction: Get a Grip On Your Business.)

"I'M A GREAT BELIEVER IN LUCK, AND I FIND THE HARDER I WORK, THE MORE I HAVE OF IT."
– THOMAS JEFFERSON

"The man who does more than he is paid for will soon be paid for more than he does."

NAPOLEON HILL

(The best-selling author of the Think & Grow Rich book series whom I named by son after. YES! I named my son Aubrey Napoleon-Hill Clark after Napoleon Hill, because the books written by Napoleon Hill changed my life. In fact, many years ago I was honored to be invited to be the keynote speaker at an event hosted in Charleston, South Carolina by the Napoleon Hill Foundation in conjunction with the Napoleon Hill Foundation and I've interviewed the best-selling author tasked with the resurrecting the unpublished writings of Napoleon Hill and the best-selling co-author of Rich Dad Poor Dad, Sharon Lechter.)

CHAPTER 40:

CREATE YOUR OWN LUCK THROUGH MASSIVE ACTION

Although I cannot control the universe and this thing called luck, I am a firm believer that you and I both can control the amount of effort that we exert on a daily basis and our attitudes. Thus, everyday I focus on the daily checklists and the small details that make the big difference. I would encourage you to pause and to reflect upon what little things you can do on a daily basis that will separate you in the workplace and in the marketplace.

"I HELP REAL BUSINESS OWNERS TO CREATE REAL SUCCESS BY IMPLEMENTING REAL SYSTEMS THAT REALLY WORK.

Motivation Is the Emotion You Receive As a Reward of Implementing the Proven Processes, Success Strategies and Best-Practice Systems That Produce Results."

"DILIGENCE, COACHABILITY, AND ATTENTION TO DETAIL ARE THE DIFFERENCE MAKERS."
- CLAY CLARK

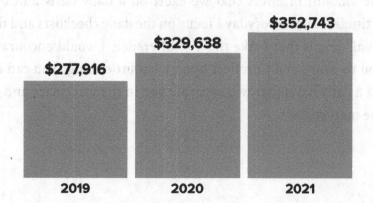

	$329,638	$352,743
$277,916		
2019	2020	2021

NATHAN & TONI SEVRINUS
OWNER / FOUNDER
www.CompleteCarpetTulsa.com

"IF YOU'RE GOING TO BE THINKING ANYTHING,
YOU MIGHT AS WELL THINK BIG."
— DONALD TRUMP

CHAPTER 41:

THINK BIG OR LIVE SMALL

"I like thinking big. If you're going to be thinking anything, you might as well think big."

PRESIDENT DONALD J. TRUMP

(President Trump is an American politician, media personality, and businessman who is the 47th president of the United States. A member of the Republican Party, he served as the 45th president from 2017 to 2021. He built his fortune developing real estate. President Donald Trump is the father of Eric Trump, who has been a frequent guest on the ThrivetimeShow.com podcast. Eric Trump is a friend of Clay Clark and has appeared at 20 conferences organized by Clay Clark).

"GREAT SPIRITS HAVE ALWAYS ENCOUNTERED
VIOLENT OPPOSITION FROM MEDIOCRE MINDS."
- ALBERT EINSTEIN

CHAPTER 42:

AVOID LOW-ENERGY, NEGATIVE & MEDIOCRE MINDS

Good energy and bad energy are both contagious. Go out of your way to avoid constant contact with negative people.

....

"Whoever walks with the wise becomes wise, but the companion of fools will suffer harm."

PROVERBS 13:20

....

"Do not be deceived: "Bad company ruins good morals."

1ST CORINTHIANS 15:33

"Great spirits have always encountered violent opposition from mediocre minds. The mediocre mind is incapable of understanding the man who refuses to bow blindly to conventional prejudices and chooses instead to express his opinions courageously and honestly."

ALBERT EINSTEIN

(A german-born theoretical physicist who developed the theory of relativity, one of the two pillars of modern physics (alongside quantum mechanics.)

"MOST ENTREPRENEURS ARE MERELY TECHNICIANS WITH AN
ENTREPRENEURIAL SEIZURE. MOST ENTREPRENEURS FAIL BECAUSE THEY ARE
WORKING IN THEIR BUSINESS RATHER THAN ON THEIR BUSINESS."
- MICHAEL GERBER

CHAPTER 43:

YOU MUST FIND TIME TO BOTH WORK ON & IN YOUR BUSINESS

Although our doors open up for business each morning six days per week, I must take time to work on the business at The Elephant In The Room Men's Grooming Lounge. Somehow in this world filled with perpetual distractions and urgent burning fires we must find the time to work on our business and not just in it.

....

"Most people today are not getting what they want. Not from their jobs, not from their families, not from their religion, not from their government, and, most importantly, not from themselves. Something is missing in most of our lives. Part of what's missing is purpose. Values."

MICHAEL GERBER

(A ThrivetimeShow.com Podcast guest, and the legendary best-selling author of The E-Myth book series)

CHAPTER 44:

NEVER LOSE MONEY

When growing and running a business your business must be profitable. In fact when running a business you will find yourself always having perpetual conflict around the following three areas:

> » **Pay - Nearly all employees want to get paid more.**

> » **Price - Nearly all customers want to pay less for the products and services a business provides.**

> » **Profit - Nearly no one on Earth other than you as the business owner cares if you are profitable or not. You must choose to be profitable or your business will fail.**

CHAPTER 45:

EVEN A GREAT PRODUCT WILL NOT SELL ITSELF

It doesn't matter how great your product or service is, it will not sell itself. You must become a master marketer if you are going to succeed in business. If you can't sell your business dreams will turn to hell. You must prioritize selling something to a real human in exchange for a real profit while consistently wowing your customers.

....

"When everything is important, nothing is important."

GINO WICKMAN

(Gino Wickman has been a multiple time guest on the ThrivetimeShow.com podcast and is known as one of the world's leading high level business consultants. He is the best-selling author of numerous books including Traction: Get a Grip On Your Business.

"ONLY ENGAGE IN MUTUALLY BENEFICIAL
RELATIONSHIPS."
- CLAY CLARK

CHAPTER 46:

ONLY ENGAGE IN WIN-WIN / MUTUALLY BENEFICIAL RELATIONSHIPS

After having spent nearly 30 years being self-employed as both a business owner and as a business growth consultant I can tell you that team work is what makes the dream work. If you are surrounded by energy vampires and soul-sucking negative influences you will eventually run out of energy and finances. You must choose to engage only in life-giving win-win relationships with your employees and your customers.

....

"A Carnegie or a Rockefeller or a James J. Hill or a Marshall Field accumulates a fortune through the application of the same principles available to all of us, but we envy them and their wealth without ever thinking of studying their philosophy and applying it to ourselves. We look at a successful person in the hour of their triumph and wonder how they did it, but we overlook the importance of analyzing their methods and we forget the price they had to pay in the careful and well-organized preparation that had to be made before they could read the fruits of their efforts."

NAPOLEON HILL

(The best-selling author of the Think & Grow Rich book series whom I named by son after. YES! I named my son Aubrey Napoleon-Hill Clark after Napoleon Hill, because the books written by Napoleon Hill changed my life. In fact, many years ago I was honored to be invited to be the keynote speaker at an event hosted in Charleston, South Carolina by the Napoleon Hill Foundation in conjunction with the Napoleon Hill Foundation and I've interviewed the best-selling author tasked with the resurrecting the unpublished writings of Napoleon Hill and the best-selling co-author of Rich Dad Poor Dad, Sharon Lechter.)

"EVERYONE HERE HAS THE SENSE THAT RIGHT
NOW IS ONE OF THOSE MOMENTS WHEN WE ARE
INFLUENCING THE FUTURE."
—STEVE JOBS

"ONLY WORK VIA APPOINTMENT."
- CLAY CLARK

CHAPTER 47:

IF EVERYTHING IS URGENT, THEN NOTHING IS IMPORTANT

If you don't consistently block out time for what matters, nothing will get done. You must learn to say no to grow. You must learn to say no to things that are not related to achieving your goals.

....

"A lot of people are afraid to tell the truth, to say no. That's where toughness comes into play. Toughness is not being a bully. It's having backbone."

 ROBERT KIYOSAKI

(A multiple-time ThrivetimeShow.com podcast guest, an author who has co-written two books with America's 45th & 47th President Donald J. Trump, the legendary best-selling author of the Rich Dad Poor Dad book series, an investor, a podcaster and a man who has actually spoken live and in-person at our Thrivetime Show business growth conference in Tulsa, Oklahoma).

CHAPTER 48:

CASUALNESS CAUSES CHAOS

In order to build a super successful business you must remember that casualness causes casualties. You must persistently fight casualness, sloppiness and the drift into disorganization on a daily basis. Every day you must make sure that checklists are completed, the files are saved properly, that doors are locked and that customers are wowed!

....

"Lack of persistence is one of the major causes of failure. Moreover, experience with thousands of people has proved that lack of persistence is a weakness common to the majority of men. It is a weakness which may be overcome with effort."

NAPOLEON HILL

The best-selling author of the Think & Grow Rich book series whom I named my son after. YES! I named my son Aubrey Napoleon-Hill Clark after Napoleon Hill, because the books written by Napoleon Hill changed my life. In fact, many years ago I was honored to be invited to be the keynote speaker at an event hosted in Charleston, South Carolina by the Napoleon Hill Foundation in conjunction with the Napoleon Hill Foundation and I've interviewed the best-selling author tasked with the resurrecting the unpublished writings of Napoleon Hill and the best-selling co-author of Rich Dad Poor Dad, Sharon Lechter.)

CHAPTER 49:

STRENGTH & GROWTH COME ONLY THROUGH CONTINUOUS EFFORT AND STRUGGLE

To become a super successful person you must commit to pushing through the pain in order to achieve the gain. If you and I are to achieve physical success in the gym our muscles must get sore. Strength can only be gained through continuous effort and struggle.

....

"To be a great Technician is simply insufficient to the task of building a great small business. Being consumed by the tactical work of the business, as every Technician suffering from an Entrepreneurial Seizure is, leads to only one thing: a complicated, frustrating, and, eventually, demeaning job!"

MICHAEL GERBER

(A ThrivetimeShow.com Podcast guest, and the legendary best-selling author of The E-Myth book series)

PLOT YOUR COURSE OR YOU WILL
NEVER GET THERE

CHAPTER 50:

A GOAL IS A DREAM WITH A DEADLINE

You must decide today that you are going to become successful and that you are going to turn your dreams into reality.

....

"I believe great people to be those who know how they got where they are, and what they need to do to get where they're going. Great people have a vision of their lives that they practice emulating each and every day. They go to work on their lives, not just in their lives. Their lives are spent living out the vision they have of their future, in the present. They compare what they've done with what they intended to do. And where there's a disparity between the two, they don't wait very long to make up the difference."

MICHAEL GERBER

(A ThrivetimeShow.com Podcast guest, and the legendary best-selling author of The E-Myth book series)

CHAPTER 51:

BUILD STRENGTH THROUGH SYSTEMS

There is only so much of you to go around. Thus you must build call scripts, email scripts, checklists, processes, recipes, blueprints, and documentation that allow for the accumulation of wealth through the scaling of WOWing your ideal and likely buyers. Focus your attention on WOWing 10 customers and then ask yourself how you can systematically WOW 100 customers. Then ask yourself how you can systemically WOW 1,000 customers.

....

"Most leaders know that bringing discipline and accountability to the organization will make people a little uncomfortable. That's an inevitable part of creating traction. What usually holds an organization back is the fear of creating this discomfort."

GINO WICKMAN

(Gino Wickman has been a multiple time guest on the ThrivetimeShow. com podcast and is known as one of the world's leading high level business consultants. He is the best-selling author of numerous books including Traction: Get a Grip On Your Business.)

"IF I HAVE SEEN FARTHER, IT IS BECAUSE I HAVE BEEN
ABLE TO STAND ON THE SHOULDERS OF GIANTS."
– SIR ISAAC NEWTON

CHAPTER 52:

SEEK PROVEN MENTORSHIP & BEST-PRACTICE SYSTEMS

You simply must commit to finding mentors who know the proven path to success if you are going to win in business. You must find people who know the best-practice systems, proven processes and success principles needed to both start and grow a successful business.

"PUT ALL OF YOUR EGGS IN ONE BASKET, AND WATCH THAT BASKET."
- ANDREW CARNEGIE

CHAPTER 53:

PUT ALL OF YOUR EGGS IN ONE BASKET

You must determine in your mind that failure is not an option if you are to succeed as an entrepreneur.

....

"A long while ago, a great warrior had to make a decision which ensured his success on the battlefield. He was about to send his armies against a powerful foe, whose men outnumbered his own. He loaded his soldiers into boats, sailed to the enemy's country, unloaded soldiers and equipment, then gave the order to burn the ships that had carried them. Addressing his men before the first battle, he said, 'You see the boats going up in smoke. That means that we cannot leave these shores alive unless we win! We now have no choice - we win or we perish!' They won. Every person who wins in any undertaking must be willing to burn his ships and cut all sources of retreat. Only by so doing can one be sure of maintaining that state of mind known as a burning desire to win, essential to success."

NAPOLEON HILL

(The best-selling author of the Think & Grow Rich book series whom I named by son after. YES! I named my son Aubrey Napoleon-Hill Clark after Napoleon Hill, because the books written by Napoleon Hill changed my life. In fact, many years ago I was honored to be invited to be the keynote speaker at an event hosted in Charleston, South Carolina by the Napoleon Hill Foundation in conjunction with the Napoleon Hill Foundation and I've interviewed the best-selling author tasked with the resurrecting the unpublished writings of Napoleon Hill and the best-selling co-author of Rich Dad Poor Dad, Sharon Lechter.)

CHAPTER 54:

DON'T REINVENT THE WHEEL

To succeed as an entrepreneur you must become a master at finding proven best-practice business systems and diligently applying these principles to your own life and business.

....

"Some people dream of success, while others wake up and work hard at it."

NAPOLEON HILL

(The best-selling author of the Think & Grow Rich book series whom I named by son after. YES! I named my son Aubrey Napoleon-Hill Clark after Napoleon Hill, because the books written by Napoleon Hill changed my life. In fact, many years ago I was honored to be invited to be the keynote speaker at an event hosted in Charleston, South Carolina by the Napoleon Hill Foundation in conjunction with the Napoleon Hill Foundation and I've interviewed the best-selling author tasked with the resurrecting the unpublished writings of Napoleon Hill and the best-selling co-author of Rich Dad Poor Dad, Sharon Lechter.)

"ALL THE SMILES IN THE WORLD AREN'T GOING
TO HELP YOU IF YOUR PRODUCT OR SERVICE IS
NOT WHAT THE CUSTOMER WANTS."
—THE SERVICE PROFIT CHAIN

CHAPTER 55:

YOU MUST WOW YOUR CUSTOMERS

....

"Deliberately seek the company of people who influence you to think and act on building the life you desire."

NAPOLEON HILL

(The best-selling author of the Think & Grow Rich book series whom I named by son after. YES! I named my son Aubrey Napoleon-Hill Clark after Napoleon Hill, because the books written by Napoleon Hill changed my life. In fact, many years ago I was honored to be invited to be the keynote speaker at an event hosted in Charleston, South Carolina by the Napoleon Hill Foundation in conjunction with the Napoleon Hill Foundation and I've interviewed the best-selling author tasked with the resurrecting the unpublished writings of Napoleon Hill and the best-selling co-author of Rich Dad Poor Dad, Sharon Lechter.)

When you WOW customers they tend to refer people very close to NOW. Go out of your way to WOW your customers and your business will improve.

THEN HE FELL ON HIS KNEES AND CRIED OUT
"LORD, DO NOT HOLD THIS SIN AGAINST THEM."
WHEN HE HAD SAID THIS, HE FELL ASLEEP
ACTS 7:60

CHAPTER 56:

IF YOU ARE A CHRISTIAN, YOU WILL BE PERSECUTED FOR RIGHTEOUSNESS SAKE

When I first became a Christian I thought that meant that I would be infinitely financially blessed and highly favored by all. From my perspective, I thought that becoming a Christian was kind of like joining a Bible-centered self-help group and that abundance and lack of adversity would become my future. However, if you and I actually read the Bible (which is the basis of Christianity) it states:

....

"Yea, and all that will live godly in Christ Jesus shall suffer persecution."

TIMOTHY 3:12

....

"If the world hates you, ye know that it hated me before it hated you."

JOHN 15:18

"10 Blessed are they which are persecuted for righteousness' sake: for theirs is the kingdom of heaven. 11 Blessed are ye, when men shall revile you, and persecute you, and shall say all manner of evil against you falsely, for my sake."

MATTHEW 5:10-11

I often keep these thoughts and facts in my mind when I am facing adversity as a result of standing up for my faith. For example, the Bible tells us in Hebrews 10:25 that you and I should not ever stop gathering and going to church on a consistent basis with other Christians.

"Not forsaking the assembling of ourselves together, as the manner of some is; but exhorting one another: and so much the more, as ye see the day approaching."

HEBREWS 10:25

And this was never a problem until the lockdowns, quarantines and curfews imposed upon us all as a result of COVID. Thus, I chose to do what I believe the Bible wants us to do and I chose to keep The Elephant In The Room Men's Grooming Lounge open for business.

The Governor of South Dakota and the United States Secretary of Homeland Security, Kristi Noem poses with a copy of my book, *Fear Unmasked* which was banned from Amazon.com because of its content. However, you can now find the book on Amazon.com.

I had a courage based upon my convictions and I happened to have friends like the late great, jewish Doctor Vladimir Zelenko, the late great muslim Doctor Rashid Buttar and the late great christian Doctor Jim Meehan that quickly knew COVID was treatable with budesonide, ivermectin and hydroxychloroquine. I also knew that the models that predicted 2.2 million Americans would die from COVID were wrong by 25 times. If you want to learn more about this visit: www.TimeToFreeAmerica.com/Revelation.

However, the point I want to communicate is that I suffered massive amounts of persecution because of my Christian faith during the lockdowns, but I was not shocked by this because the Bible promises that as Christians we will be persecuted for our faith.

NOT-SO-FUN FACTS:

HOW THE APOSTLES DIED.

» 1. Matthew - Matthew suffered martyrdom in Ethiopia, Killed by a sword wound.

» 2. Mark - Mark died in Alexandria, Egypt, after being dragged by Horses through the streets until he was dead.

» 3. Luke was hanged in Greece as a result of his tremendous preaching to the lost.

» 4. John - John faced martyrdom when he was boiled in a huge Basin of boiling oil during a wave of persecution In Rome. However, he was miraculously delivered from death. John was then sentenced to the mines on the prison Island of Patmos. He wrote his prophetic Book of Revelation on

Patmos. The apostle John was later freed and returned to serve as Bishop of Edessa in modern Turkey. He died as an old man, the only apostle to die peacefully

» 5. Peter - He was crucified upside down on an x-shaped cross. According to church tradition it was because he told his tormentors that he felt unworthy to die In the same way that Jesus Christ had died.

» 6. James - The leader of the church in Jerusalem, was thrown over a hundred feet down from the southeast pinnacle of the Temple when he refused to deny his faith in Christ. When they discovered that he survived the fall, his enemies beat James to death with a fuller's club. This was the same pinnacle where Satan had taken Jesus during the Temptation.

» 7. James - The Son of Zebedee, was a fisherman by trade when Jesus Called him to a lifetime of ministry. As a strong leader of the church, James was beheaded at Jerusalem. The Roman officer who guarded James watched amazed as James defended his faith at his trial. Later, the officer walked beside James to the place of execution. Overcome by conviction, he declared his new faith to the judge and Knelt beside James to accept beheading as a Christian.

» 8. Bartholomew - Also known as Nathaniel was a missionary to Asia. He witnessed for our Lord in present-day Turkey. Bartholomew was martyred for his preaching in Armenia where he was flayed to death by a whip.

» 9. Andrew - Andrew was crucified on an x-shaped cross in Patras, Greece. After being whipped severely by seven soldiers they tied his body to the cross with cords to prolong his agony. His followers reported that, when he was led toward the cross, Andrew saluted it in these words: 'I have long desired and expected this happy hour. The cross has been consecrated by the body of Christ hanging on it.' He continued to preach to his tormentors for two days until he expired.

» 10. Thomas - Thomas was stabbed with a spear in India during one of his missionary trips to establish the church in the Sub-continent.

» 11. Jude - Jude was killed with arrows when he refused to deny his faith in Christ.

» 12. Matthias - Matthias, the apostle chosen to replace the traitor Judas Iscariot, was stoned and then beheaded.

» 13. Paul - Paul was tortured and then beheaded by the evil Emperor Nero at Rome in A.D. 67. Paul endured a lengthy imprisonment, which allowed him to write his many epistles to the churches he had formed throughout the Roman Empire.

I inserted the following troubling information about how the Apostles died (those that were closest to Jesus) as a reminder to us that our sufferings here on Earth are indeed minor compared to the intense persecution and cold cruelty faced by the apostles and disciples during their times for the sake of the Faith.

• Why do we feel sleepy in prayer, but yet we are able to stay awake as we watch a non-sensical comedy?

_____

• Why are we so bored when we look at the HOLY BOOK, but find it easy to read other books?

_____

Listed below I have provided a plethora, a buffet and a large amount of resources and tools that I believe you will find helpful as you pursue success:

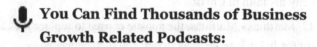 **You Can Find Thousands of Business Growth Related Podcasts:**

» https://www.thrivetimeshow.com/podcast-guests/
» Thrivetime Show on Spotify
» Thrivetime Show on iTunes

You Can Find All 35+ Books That I Have Ever Written to Download for Free Today At:

» www.ThrivetimeShow.com/Free-Resources

As An Elephant In The Room Men's Grooming Lounge Member, You Can Claim Your Free Thrivetime Show 2-Day Interactive Business Growth Conference Ticket Today At:

www.ThrivetimeShow.com or You May Text Me Directly to Request a Ticket At: 918-851-0102

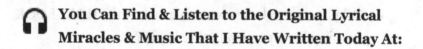 **You Can Find & Listen to the Original Lyrical Miracles & Music That I Have Written Today At:**

www.ThrivetimeShow.com/Lyrical-Miracles

You Can Find Thousands of Faith Building Client Success Stories & Case Studies Today At: www.ThrivetimeShow.com/Testimonials

You Can Experience the Online Entrepreneurship School That I Built At: www.Thrive15.com

You Can Find a Treasure Trove of Best-Practice Business Systems & Processes Free to Download Today At:

www.ThrivetimeShow.com/Downloadables

"Life is not a dress rehearsal. The time for you to turn your big dreams into reality will never be just right. You must act now!"

- Clay Clark

WANT TO KNOW EVEN MORE?
CHECK OUT ALL OF CLAY'S BOOKS

HOW TO BUILD A SUCCESSFUL BUSINESS

The World's Best Business Growth & Consulting Book: Business Growth Strategies from the World's Best Business Coach.

PODCAST DOMINATION 101

This book will show you how to prepare, record, launch, and begin generating income from your podcast, all from your home studio!

TRADE-UPS

Learn how to design and live the life you love, how to find and create the time needed to get things done in a world filled with endless digital distractions, and more!

THE ENTREPRENEUR'S DRAGON ENERGY

The Mindset Kanye, Trump and You Need to Succeed.

THRIVE

How to Take Control of Your Destiny and Move Beyond Surviving... Now!

JACKASSARY

Jackassery will serve as a beacon of light for other entrepreneurs that are looking to avoid troublesome employees and difficult situations. This is real. This is raw. This is unfiltered entrepreneurship.

BOOM

The 14 Proven Steps to Business Success.

SEARCH ENGINE DOMINATION

Learn the Proven System We've Used to Earn Millions.

FEAR UNMASKED

Fear Unmasked gives you the essential information you need to know about the coronavirus, the government shutdown, and the media that is perpetuating the hysteria.

IT'S NOT LONELY AT THE TOP

15 Keys to achieving a successful, peaceful, and drama-free life. (3/4 of this book is handwritten by Clay Clark, himself).

HOW TO REPEL FRIENDS AND NOT INFLUENCE PEOPLE

The epic whale of a tale featuring America's self proclaimed most humble male.

HOW TO BUILD A SUCCESSFUL BUSINESS

In This Game Changing & Life Changing Book You Will Learn the Proven Processes, Success Strategies, and Secrets to Unlocking Your Potential While Learning the Following & More:

HOW TO BUILD A SUCCESSFUL BUSINESS

In This Game Changing & Life Changing Book You Will Learn the Proven Processes, Success Strategies, and Secrets to Unlocking Your Potential While Learning the Following & More:

FEAR UNMASKED 2.0

Updated and revised for 2021. Fear Unmasked 2.0 provides more resources to kill the spirit of fear and giving YOU an action plan to save America.

BELICHICK: AN UNAUTHORIZED LOOK UNDER THE HOODIE

Many fans enthusiastically cheer for the EPIC teams assembled and coached by Coach Bill Belichick.

CREATING HABITUAL WEALTH

Learn the proven path to creating financial success.

F6 JOURNAL

Meta Thrive Time Journal.

FEAR UNMASKED

Fear Unmasked gives you the essential information you need to know about the coronavirus, the government shutdown, and the media that is perpetuating the hysteria.

HOW TO BECOME SUSTAINABLY RICH

In This Game Changing & Life Changing Book You Will Learn the Proven Processes, Success Strategies, and Secrets to Unlocking Your Potential While Learning the Following & More:

WILL NOT WORK FOR FOOD

9 Big Ideas for Effectively Managing Your Business in an Increasingly Dumb, Distracted & Dishonest America.

THE ART OF POWERFUL PUBLIC SPEAKING

In this page-turning power-packed classic, Clay Clark teams up with the (now deceased) long-time friend and speaking mentor Carlton Pearson to teach you proven public speaking tips, tricks, and moves that you can use.

SALES DOMINATION

Clay Clark is a master of selling and now he wants to teach you his proven processes, scalable systems and sales mastery moves in a humorous and practical way.

THE ELEPHANT IN THE ROOM

In this action-focused guide, Clay Clark gives you a proven plan to fast-track you to success!

THE ART OF GETTING THINGS DONE

Clay Clark breaks down the proven, time-tested and time freedom creating super moves that you can use to create both the time freedom and financial freedom that most people only dream about.

THE HOMO DEUCE

This book was written to provide you with a POWERFUL TOOL to help you wake up your family and friends to "The Great Reset" and "Fourth Industrial Revolution" agenda

WHEEL OF WEALTH

An Entrepreneur's Action Guide.

MAKE YOUR LIFE EPIC

Clay shares his journey and struggle from the dorm room to the board room during his raw and action-packed story of how he built DJConnection.com.

HOW TO HIRE QUALITY EMPLOYEES

This candid book shares how to avoid being held hostage by employees.

THE GREAT RESET VERSUS THE GREAT AWAKENING

The Great Reset Versus The Great Awakening breaks down this EPIC battle between good and evil.

IF MY WALLS COULD TALK

The Notes, Quotes, & Epiphanies I've Written On Clay's Office Walls. (Hardcover).

Legendary best-selling author, investor, podcaster, and entrepreneur, Robert Kiyosaki speaking at CLay Clark's business growth conference in Tulsa, Ok.

www.ingramcontent.com/pod-product-compliance
Lightning Source LLC
Chambersburg PA
CBHW010811140625
28089CB00005B/15